MANIFEST

YOUR

INFINITE

RICHES

Pushkar Anand

CENTRE FOR INFINITE RICHES
Keep Growing . . . . .

https://www.centreforinfiniteriches.com

Text © 2025 Pushkar Anand
Cover Design © 2025 Alex Mansfield
All rights reserved.

First published 2025
by Rowanvale Books Ltd
The Gate
Keppoch Street
Roath
Cardiff
CF24 3JW
https://www.rowanvalebooks.com

A CIP catalog record for this book is available from the British Library.
ISBN: 978-1-83584-043-6

Print and bound in Great Britain by Bell & Bain Ltd, Glasgow

DEDICATED TO

——————————————→

KARAN ANAND
MY FATHER

&

BLAINE BARTLETT
(GRANDMASTER B^2)
MY TEACHER

←——————————————

INTRODUCTION

Yes, you are infinitely rich; you are infinitely rich because you are you!

Ignore your bank balance, worldly possessions and other "traditional" means of gauging wealth – look within yourself and you will find everything you need to manifest your deepest aspirations.

The purpose of this book is to help you find the truest expression of your own infinite riches. That can mean whatever level of material wealth or money you desire, as well as living in harmony with your distinctive spirit.

We are often brought up to believe that successful people are cut from a different cloth, that some special people are just lucky, and that some mysterious factor outside our control determines how successful we are. This book will help you learn why you are entirely in command of your own success and what you need to do to achieve that success.

Never again will you feel that something you truly desire is out of your reach – whether that's the kind of home you have your heart set on, the abundant finances you want in your account, or the person you'd really like to be. The form of your desires is secondary; what is primary is to facilitate a significant shift within you, which will put you on the path to living the life you really want.

Human nature is such that once you know something can be done, half the journey is complete; the other half is about successful application and disciplined execution. My conviction comes from my own journey spanning fifteen years and from the people I have worked closely with over the years, as well as other people whose life stories are relatively well known. You will hear more about them and my story as you read through these pages.

Think of this book as a manual to transform your world; a guide to help you progress from the life you currently live to the life you really want to live. Along this journey, you will learn "new to you" concepts and see other ideas already familiar to you in a different light. Understanding these concepts and ideas is the critical first step, but this in itself will not get you the results; consistent application in putting them to practical use and ensuring disciplined execution are the decisive factors.

Most importantly, as you will learn after reading this book, authentic learning – which enables you to act on knowledge distilled deep inside you – comes through repetition. Truly valuable books are not one-off reads but constant companions, which you read and refer to on an ongoing basis. It is my sincere desire and intention that this book serves this purpose in your life.

FOREWORD

The stories we tell ourselves about ourselves are an important component of our success. In *Manifest Your Infinite Riches*, you will learn in a liberating and transformative manner how to make the most of your inner abundance and live your infinitely rich life. It reminds me of something I witnessed almost forty years ago, which is a wonderful example of how we can think our way to success.

I met a young boy I'll call Johnny, who was only about seven years old. I was at an impromptu picnic by a small river with a couple of friends. The riverbank rose about one meter above the water, and Johnny had wandered over to the edge, picking up rocks and tossing them in. His father, mother, and younger sister sat about seven meters away under a grove of trees, having lunch and watching him.

At one point, Johnny's father called out, "Johnny, come away from the bank, you're going to fall in." Johnny heard him but kept reaching down, picking up rocks and tossing them into the water. Louder this time, his father repeated, "Johnny, I said come away from the riverbank, you're going to fall in!" Johnny, however, continued to throw rocks into the river.

After a few more warnings, his father walked over to him, saying in an exasperated tone, "I'm not going to tell you again. Step away from the bank, you're going to fall in." Finally, Johnny stopped, looked up at his father, and said, "Daddy, that's your fear, not mine." His dad paused, then leaned down, picked up a rock, and the two of them spent some time together, tossing rocks into the river.

For decades now, I have championed the belief that the greatest and most authentic wealth resides not in our bank accounts, but within ourselves. We are all infinitely rich, endowed with unique talents, abilities, and a potential far greater than any material measure. Yet most of us hesitate to access those gifts because, somewhere along the way, we too were told to "step away from the bank." Over time, these treasures within us become hidden or even forgotten.

In *Manifest Your Infinite Riches*, Pushkar highlights this truth and presents a powerful blueprint for recognizing and unlocking our inherent abundance. This book goes far beyond traditional paradigms of wealth creation, which often focus on competition, scarcity, and external validation. Instead, it guides you on a journey of self-discovery, encouraging alignment with your soul's purpose – your Primary Mission – and outlining a creation process that results in making a significant impact on your life, to the benefit of everyone.

The principles and practices outlined in this book truly empower you to first recognize and then become the person you were always meant to be, while aligning your energy with the frequency of abundance. Pushkar's own experiences and insights (including his founding of the **Centre for Infinite Riches**®), as well as the examples of many others, light the way, offering a practical and inspiring roadmap to living a life filled with purpose, intellectual, spiritual and material contentment, and prosperity.

This book is not merely a guide to accumulating wealth, but a journey of self-evolution much beyond one's present state. It challenges you to examine your beliefs, tap into your innate creativity, and step into a life of greater purpose and meaning. As you embrace these concepts and apply the techniques shared here, you'll attract not only financial abundance but also experience a profound shift in consciousness and a deeper connection to your true self.

Blaine Bartlett (Grandmaster B²)

TABLE OF CONTENTS

PART I

---→

RECOGNIZE YOUR INFINITE RICHES

←---

1.
MONEY

1. MONEY

I never did it for the money. Being the richest man in the cemetery doesn't matter to me. Going to bed at night saying we've done something wonderful, that's what matters to me.

Steve Jobs

I have this quotation framed on my desk. Every time I see it, I am reminded of an enterprise valued at $3.4 trillion that has positively impacted more than two billion people and continues to contribute to our lives every day. Yet, its founder, Steve Jobs, never did it for money. This indeed is a powerful lesson for us all.

One of the most influential philosophers of our time, Bob Proctor, who was Chairman of the Proctor Gallagher Institute until his passing in February 2022, often said *the key to creating wealth for yourself is to understand that money is not the goal.* Bob's enterprise elevated millions of people across the world in his lifetime and continues to do so now.

Likewise, as you set out on the journey to manifest your infinite riches, I want money to play the same role in your life. However, that does not mean money is not relevant; on the contrary, it is enormously relevant, and must be correctly slotted in its rightful place.

I have placed this chapter on **Money** at the beginning of the book because it is monumentally important for you to truly appreciate the role money plays and the place it occupies as you start the process to manifest your infinite riches. There is a subsequent chapter titled **Money, Money, Money: Is It Really About The Money?** where you will learn all about **The Six Statutes of Money**™.

At this point however, I would like you to have some context on the role of money to carry forward with you as you read through this book, and so, giving you a sneak peek, I am introducing you to one of these Statutes, **The Rules of Receiving Money**.

This statute, **The Rules of Receiving Money**, says that the money you receive in exchange for providing products/services depends on:

(i) Whether your underlying intention is to "Give" an exceptional product/service experience or to "Get" the maximum amount of money.

(ii) Your purpose, and whether the products/services adequately represent your purpose.

(iii) What the most distinctive characteristics of your products/services are.

To give you an example, I am sharing the answers to these questions for Apple Inc. when Steve Jobs co-founded it in 1976:

(i) To "Give".

(ii) To make a contribution to the world by making tools for the mind that advance humankind.

(iii) Change the way people view computers by developing user-friendly versions small enough for people to have in their homes or offices.

Now take a moment and think about the multitude of people who go about their daily lives in this ocean of humanity we live in. You will notice that the vast majority do the work they do with the primary objective of earning money. Paradoxically, despite this driver, they almost always still need more money than they earn!

Conversely, there are those whose work is their passion and an extension of their core purpose. Not all such people are luminaries of their respective fields like Steve Jobs and Bob Proctor, but they undoubtedly lead more abundant lives than the majority. It so happens that when you have this wider alignment with your inherent purpose and it is supplemented with doing certain things in certain ways, a universal force magically encircles your life… and you never again lack money.

Heart of the Matter

While money is not the destination, it is extremely pertinent to your journey, and it is important to position it in the right place while your enterprise focuses on positively impacting everyone it serves.

2.
YOUR INFINITE RICHES

2. YOUR INFINITE RICHES

Genius is a potential that lives within you and every other human being. I'd like you to consider what might seem like a radical idea: Genius can show up in as many ways as there are human beings.

Wayne Dyer

Can you remember how it felt when someone you didn't know very well casually said, "You're so good at that"? Or the feeling you had when a particular task immediately filled you with a sense of purpose, focus, and a desire to really excel? Or the immense satisfaction of doing a certain activity, in which you lost track of time and the actions flowed naturally and effortlessly?

Each of these situations would be examples of you tapping into your natural-born genius, your innate and unique talent, your infinite riches. Each and every one of us has these in abundance. For some people, their riches are buried deep, barely surfacing to be acknowledged or understood; for others, they manifest daily, garnering admiration all around.

My primary objective in this book is to put you in the driver's seat so you can draw from the well of your infinite riches, manifest daily the exclusive talent you were born with, and thereby live in harmony with your soul. By tapping into your infinite riches, you can achieve whatever you want – be it financial abundance, career progression, a desired lifestyle, or the perfect expression of your own happiness.

For it is in giving, that we receive.

St Francis of Assisi

As you read through the pages that follow, I want you to really understand – and make it a way of life – that by recognizing your very own infinite riches and harmonizing with them, your primary focus is to manifest your infinite riches, to give them physical form.

When that happens, through the nature of your enterprise – the work you do – you enrich everyone whom your work touches. As a result, your infinite riches benefit you as well, in direct alignment with the extent to which your work benefits others. Your deepest wishes, however, can only be fulfilled if, while expressing your genius, you originate from a place of generosity with a genuine desire to positively impact everyone you serve.

When blended together, the power of generosity, the mindset of giving, and the quality of compassion create a positive ripple effect, opening the door to more abundance for all involved. When I started to live my purpose to uplift humanity, the overarching sentiment in my heart was about how I could benefit the people I was interacting with.

This sentiment has consistently remained paramount as I've continued on this journey and started to interact with more and more people with every passing year. Eventually, what started as a tiny venture with a handful of people, took on a life of its own and metamorphosed into my writing this book for readers globally and founding my enterprise, which has grown to a presence in every continent.

The principal point to grasp here is that the feeling generated within me at every successful step was such that I was overwhelmed with gratitude and humility, often with a lump in my throat rather than an ego-driven sense of achievement.

This feeling I refer to is one where you are on this path you know you were meant to follow, you cherish every moment of it, and you gradually make it a way of life. This in turn transforms your life such that you are living your foremost purpose, benefiting everyone you interact with, and setting in motion the forces that ensure your financial freedom. In other words, you start to manifest your infinite riches.

Heart of the Matter

Manifesting your infinite riches beautifully enables the advancement of both the provider (you) and all those you serve through your enterprise.

3.
YOU ARE SPECIAL

3. YOU ARE SPECIAL

To be yourself in a world that is constantly trying to make you something else is the greatest accomplishment.

Ralph Waldo Emerson

Just as every human being is a genius within but only few reflect that genius outwards, so too, while every human being is infinitely rich, only few manifest their infinite riches. We can either look on with envy or – as I did in 2008 – we can start trying to understand our position in the world and what we can change.

By the age of thirty, I had got to a place in my life wherein, by most barometers, I was considered successful: employed with what was then the world's most global bank, happily married with the first child on their way, and the wider family living close by. But the 2007-8 global financial crisis made me question the validity of my choices. On the face of it, I was set up for life; but was it really my life or the life that everyone else presumed I'd want?

My answer was simple: I encashed every penny I had and headed off to Cambridge with wife and infant in tow to attend the MBA program and start afresh thereafter. Everyone said I was insane to give up my career and be in debt to the tune of $100,000. I still did it, because I wanted to, and my inner voice nudged me on. Despite having made my choice, there were these repetitive questions inside me that really started to haunt me at this stage – questions that had only occasionally troubled me in my twenties.

Why are some people successful and others not? Is it all about luck? Or is it about intelligence? Do we even know whether we create our reality, or are we helpless in the hands of an external power? Does where we are born make a difference? What role does education play? What about family?

Such questions lingered for days on end, fired by their own energy – persistently, determinedly, relentlessly urging me to seek answers, to discover secrets, to solve the riddle. These questions tormented me with such intensity, especially against the backdrop of the global financial crisis and the major shift in my life, that they played a pivotal part in my decision to explore and to educate myself to understand the potential within every human being, and what was needed to tap into that potential.

My quest took fifteen hard-working, deep-studying, and thoughtful years. I read about 500 books, enrolled in thirty-or-so seminars and workshops, and spent four years in a one-to-one learning model with Blaine Bartlett, my teacher, whom I fondly refer to as Grandmaster B², and to whom I owe more gratitude than anyone else in the field of personal development. He in turn had spent more than thirty-five years developing his knowledge, understanding, and mastery of the nature of our inner gifts.

As well as gaining a deeper perspective, I started to notice things about where my insights and personal progress came from. On each occasion that I felt I had made a step forward or fulfilled a deeply-held wish, I realized it was on the back of diligently following a certain method of doing specific things in exact ways.

Over the course of my journey, I took numerous opportunities to discuss with others on the same journey their pathways to knowledge. It became evident that their experiences, responses, and discoveries were consistent with each other's and with mine.

I would describe everyone I discussed these things with as "ordinary people", though drawn from different walks of life and varied cultures. It made me realize: if every human being were given the opportunity to gain and apply the knowledge we had developed, then they too could have whatever it is they desired.

From my study of Bob Proctor's, *You Were Born Rich*, I came to understand that every human being is born rich because we are born with the ability to have whatever we want within the bounds of nature.

My wider studies and research also helped me recognize that the reason some fulfill their desires while others don't, boils down not to what you are born with but instead to the absence of – or access to – this precise knowledge which took me fifteen years to gather and assimilate. It so happens that the education system around the world, while of course imparting valuable lessons, does not even touch upon this knowledge, which my own studies opened up to me.

Remember though, despite being infinitely rich, unless you have learnt what specifically needs to be done on an ongoing basis, why it needs to be done, and exactly how to do it, these riches won't manifest. Instead, they will remain more like the treasure buried in the backyard that you didn't know about. As you gain the relevant knowledge (why) and instill the discipline to do specific things in exact ways (what and how), you will then recognize and develop your unique and magnificent talent – or the genius within you.

The "Impression of Increase" is a powerful concept set forth in Wallace Wattles' seminal work, *The Science of Getting Rich*, at the start of the 20th century. Wattles was a New Thought writer and, amongst other topics, he wrote about the importance of how we must leave everyone we serve in an enhanced state compared to before we served them. New Thought as a concept explains how your thoughts, beliefs, and mind shape your physical reality.

As I dug deeper into the archives of New Thought, I often received valuable guidance and reinforcement. In this context, the synchronicity I found in one of Wayne Dyer's last books, *I Can See Clearly Now*, is indeed noteworthy. Written in semi-autobiographical form, this book seemed to time and again share with me experiences of his life which were most applicable to mine.

For example, in the early-mid-1970s, about three or four years before Wayne's first book, *Your Erroneous Zones,* was published and when Wayne was not widely known, he says he often thought to himself:

> *I've read Dale Carnegie, Napoleon Hill and Norman Vincent Peale and feel that I can offer a book that goes beyond their inspiration and advice. I love and admire all of these men and what they have offered – I see them as pioneers in a fascinating club I intend to join.*

If I were to replace Dale Carnegie, Napoleon Hill, and Norman Vincent Peale with Bob Proctor, Jack Canfield, and Wayne Dyer himself, those thoughts would seem just like mine – particularly over the last few years.

Moreover, going with the flow of his callings to write full-time and cater to the general public – which was an unknown for him then – meant transitioning from his cushy job in academia and the security of the monthly salary inflow. He says:

> *This was a plum of a job to be sure, yet there was something burning inside me, demanding my full-time attention. My outer world looked great, but my inner world, where I do all of my living, felt incomplete and restless.*

Again, this was as applicable to me as it was to Wayne. These were some of the insights that laid the foundation of the **Centre for Infinite Riches**®. And now, like those who walked the path before me, I am writing a guide to help others uncover the knowledge they need and the actions they should take to manifest their infinite riches.

Heart of the Matter

Although the longing to know more is still there, and the never-ending journey of study continues, this book covers the answers I found over fifteen years. Voraciously read and follow the learnings here – they will help you identify and manifest your infinite riches much quicker than the time it took me to manifest mine!

4.
UNLEARN WHAT YOU'VE LEARNT

4. UNLEARN WHAT YOU'VE LEARNT

Conformity is the jailer of freedom and the enemy of growth.

John F. Kennedy

One percent of the world's population owns forty-five percent of global wealth, while the next twelve percent owns forty percent. At the other end of the spectrum, fifty-two percent of the world's population owns as little as one percent of global wealth.

The question any right-thinking person would ask is: "Why is there such a mammoth difference between clusters of the same population of human beings?" This disparity is even starker when you consider that every human being is infinitely rich.

The answer sounds simple: the absence of awareness. Recognizing this absence and then effecting personal change takes a significant shift as an individual. Understanding how we are conditioned to think and to live was a major part of my research. We live in a world that celebrates conformity, and yet that conformity restricts the authenticity of so many people.

As we move from childhood through school to adulthood and eventually to the workplace, our outlook on life is strongly influenced and conditioned by the outlook of those around us. Unfortunately, most of those around us – the wider society or ecosystem – are stuck; stuck in the Daily Rut Rat-Race Bubble – or the DR^3 Bubble, from hereon.

Spending more time with others over the course of our life causes their views to become our views, their lack to become our lack, and their thinking to become our thinking. As time goes by, we become more engulfed within this bubble and, without realizing, this causes more people to do the same. Without meaning to, most of humanity contributes to growing this bubble exponentially, like the Covid R rate during the pandemic.

Yet, there is a minority of the population spread around the world who, either consciously or otherwise, have claimed their infinite riches and live infinitely rich lives. This is not because they are superior or special in any way; it is just that they have the awareness of being infinitely rich and this reflects in their manifestation experiences.

Often the sole reason for them having this awareness is because a family member, a parent, or a teacher consciously worked to feed this awareness into them during their formative years. A worthwhile example that comes to mind here is the popular book *Rich Dad Poor Dad* where, amongst other things, the author explains how his awareness of wealth began through a rich dad (the father of his best friend), when he was nine years old.

On the contrary, the author's own father – poor dad – could not answer his questions about what one needs to do to be wealthy. You see, his father was representative of most parents and people in the world, who lack the knowledge and clarity to answer what one needs to do to become wealthy while leading a fulfilling life. It is because there is such a dearth of this perspective of how to live an abundant life that most people, generation after generation, accept the fact that "lack" is a fundamental part of life.

Another route to infinite riches is when we remain open-minded and receptive – we hear a whisper, its voice gets louder and stronger, eventually leading us to act on it. In turn, this action leads us to a source, which can help us rekindle the spark at will. An apt example in this case would be you finding your way to this book. It is possible you believe you did not consciously look for this book but that, coincidentally, it found its way to you. Even if you were not conscious of a desire within you, it does not mean the desire was not there. If this sounds like a new concept to you, rest assured, you will learn more about it as you read through these pages. Remember, there are no coincidences. As the great Persian poet, Rumi, said almost 1,000 years ago, *What you seek also seeks you.*

If you think what I am saying is beside the point and the family and circumstances you were born into are the primary factors that determine your life's path, you'd be wrong – believe me, profoundly wrong. I understand your reasoning because that is how I thought for a good many years! However, this thinking is entirely down to your conditioning and what you have been exposed to over the years; how you have been swayed by friends, family, wider society, and the media, and eventually habituated to this view.

Now ask yourself – isn't it natural to say that if your life's trajectory were based primarily on where you were born, then everyone born into the same family or neighborhood would have very similar, if not the same, results in life? More so, if this were true, then logically, there would be no new billionaires, centi-millionaires, or millionaires! If you are wondering whether it is only the rarest of cases that defy the norm, or that they are all merely lucky coincidences, then pay careful attention to what follows because it will help your breakthrough to infinite riches.

An exception is anything that is a deviation from the norm. Yes, the examples you think of are exceptions, but these are not coincidental exceptions that just happened – as people often wrongly believe. Instead, these are exceptions which manifested because the people behind them either consciously or otherwise gained the specific expertise you are being introduced to in this book.

Because a small number of arbitrary people did this successfully does not make it a coincidence but, instead, reinforces the point that anyone can do it. The challenge is not in people's ability to do it but in getting people en masse to access the material in this book, so they develop this awareness and act on it. In the process, the exception will then start to become the norm and, in the overall scheme of things, humankind will evolve to a higher level.

Heart of the Matter

You don't have to conform – start to get familiar with the idea of doing what you want to do, and not what others think you should do!

PART II

→

UNLOCK YOUR INFINITE RICHES

←

5.
THE MULTI-PRONGED MODEL TO MANIFEST YOUR INFINITE RICHES™

5. THE MULTI-PRONGED MODEL TO MANIFEST YOUR INFINITE RICHES™

If you can't explain it simply, you don't understand it well enough.

Albert Einstein

My intention in this chapter is for you to know what you must gain mastery over to manifest your infinite riches. Ideally, by the end of reading this book, I would like you to be comfortable enough to be able to explain this process simply to anyone.

The knowledge you need to assimilate is summarized in the Multi-Pronged Model which follows. It is a simple model, but don't underestimate its capability. Simple does not mean easy. Truly understanding and internalizing the model is not easy because it is new to you and some of its features will require you to change the way you have looked at things in the past. Open-mindedness, a genuine desire to grow, and discipline will all contribute to you attaining mastery.

The Multi-Pronged Model

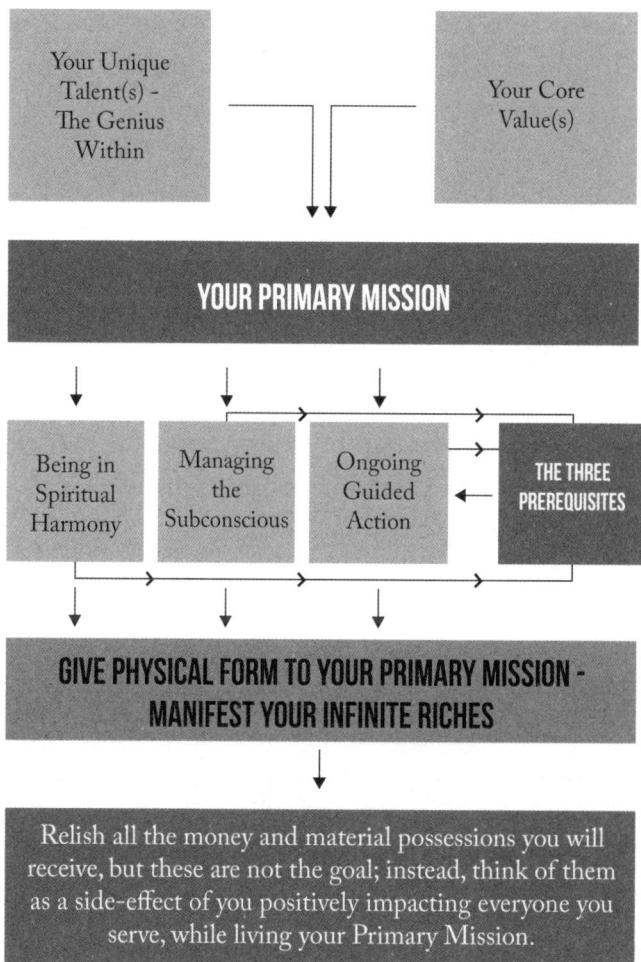

```
┌──────────────────┐                    ┌──────────────────┐
│ Your Unique      │                    │                  │
│ Talent(s) -      │────────────┐       │ Your Core        │
│ The Genius       │            │       │ Value(s)         │
│ Within           │            ▼▼      │                  │
└──────────────────┘                    └──────────────────┘

┌──────────────────────────────────────────────────────────┐
│              YOUR PRIMARY MISSION                          │
└──────────────────────────────────────────────────────────┘
     │            │              │
     ▼            ▼              ▼
┌─────────┐ ┌──────────┐ ┌──────────┐      ┌──────────────┐
│ Being in│ │ Managing │ │ Ongoing  │      │ THE THREE    │
│ Spiritual│ │ the     │ │ Guided   │ ◄─── │ PREREQUISITES│
│ Harmony │ │Subconscious│ │ Action │      │              │
└─────────┘ └──────────┘ └──────────┘      └──────────────┘
     │            │              │
     ▼            ▼              ▼
┌──────────────────────────────────────────────────────────┐
│   GIVE PHYSICAL FORM TO YOUR PRIMARY MISSION -            │
│         MANIFEST YOUR INFINITE RICHES                     │
└──────────────────────────────────────────────────────────┘
                        │
                        ▼
┌──────────────────────────────────────────────────────────┐
│ Relish all the money and material possessions you will    │
│ receive, but these are not the goal; instead, think of them│
│ as a side-effect of you positively impacting everyone you │
│ serve, while living your Primary Mission.                 │
└──────────────────────────────────────────────────────────┘
```

The first step is to identify both your unique talent(s) and your core value(s). These then come together to define your Primary Mission; you can use the terms Primary Purpose and Primary Mission interchangeably.

Once your Primary Mission has been identified, the next step is to ensure that you are successfully living your Primary Mission. This, in turn, means that not only is this mission in spiritual harmony but that the subconscious is actively managed, and you are consistently taking Ongoing Guided Action.

By virtue of fulfilling these requirements, you then become the vehicle that gives physical form to your Primary Mission. In other words, you manifest your Primary Mission. The form your Primary Mission takes is defined as your Primary Vision. In everyday language, you can also think of your Primary Vision as synonymous with your principal goal.

The rest of **Part II: Unlock Your Infinite Riches** helps you thoroughly grasp each of the components of this model and includes numerous real-life examples. It also takes you step-by-step through a set of exercises so that you derive your very own Primary Mission and Vision.

It is crucial, though, that you first conscientiously understand the key concepts at play here, read through the real-life examples and methodically do the exercises before you define your Primary Mission and Vision; and this is exactly what you'll do in the subsequent chapters.

However, to give you an initial flavor, I am sharing the story of a dear friend of mine, Dave Murphy, whom I have known since 2011 when he became my financial advisor.

Dave used to work with a large accountancy firm. When the firm wound down in 2015, Dave and another former colleague set up their own practice. The practice started to grow and did well, but in early 2018, Dave got the shock of his life when he learnt that his trusted partner was cheating on him and siphoning funds. After a tumultuous year, Dave extricated himself from that firm, receiving only half the money due to him.

Towards the latter part of 2019, using his life savings and settlement funds, Dave successfully established a new firm with a small set of loyal clients and simultaneously set up a confectionery shop in his neighborhood on the outskirts of Manchester. In his own words: "Pushkar, I just loved the satisfaction I got from providing delicious sweets in my shop to different people, seeing the day go by and chatting with them… I felt alive again. I am also enjoying my new practice working with a select set of like-minded clients."

Unfortunately, just as things were consolidating again, Covid struck. The confectionery shop shut down and, as a self-employed financial advisor, while the practice continued, life was severely disrupted yet again. To cut a long story short, through a chain of well-meaning and positive events over the last three years, Dave is now one of the three partners of a thriving firm – https://www.howebridgeconsulting.co.uk

The other two have a similar set of values to his but, most importantly, Dave is the partner responsible for managing the finances of the firm!

As recently as early 2024, Dave and I were chatting about the Multi-Pronged Model and got down to a preliminary version of his Primary Mission and Vision. These were the answers we agreed on:

- ➢ **Dave's unique talent(s):** Accountancy and financial management, baking and cooking confectionery and other sweet foods, and counseling.
- ➢ **Dave's core values(s):** Honesty, loyalty, and compassion.
- ➢ **Primary Mission:** Minimize or eliminate people's hassles.
- ➢ **Primary Vision:** By December 31, 2026 - my firm (https://www.howebridgeconsulting.co.uk) has 500 clients, the confectionery shop has re-opened, serving at least twenty-five customers every day, and I devote six hours a week to counseling homeless people.

Heart of the Matter

Mastering the Multi-Pronged Model will leave you with an invaluable foundation to manifest your infinite riches.

6.
PRIMARY MISSION
& VISION

6. PRIMARY MISSION & VISION

The minute you choose to do what you really want to do, it's a different kind of life.

Bucky Fuller

There are quite a few well-written books (my favorite is *Your Soul's Plan*) which credibly discuss the idea that before conception – when in soul form – you decide on the principal objectives for your time on earth. Objectives is in the plural because there are multiple avenues of life, such as parenting, career, friendship, spousal relationships, etc., and each has a focal objective. Across all these, however, there is one overarching objective – the Primary Mission – which does not have to be in the career sphere, but often is, and this is our focus.

Conceptually, the form you would like any mission to take when it manifests is the vision, and the vision that corresponds to the Primary Mission is the Primary Vision.

The Mission-Vision Framework

One of my cherished quotations is Wayne Dyer's on the concept of *Dharma*:

We all have a destiny, a dharma to fulfill, and there are endless opportunities, people, and circumstances that surface throughout our lives to illuminate our path. The incidents and the people create tiny sparks that cause us to recognize, this is for me—this is important; [...] That inner spark is God talking to me, and I simply refuse to ignore it. I know that if I feel it and it ignites something in me, then the igniting process is the invisible, the Source, the very essence of all creation—and I trust it to the max.

The term *Dharma* comes from Hindu philosophy and is sometimes translated into English as "religion"; this is wrong. The correct translation of *Dharma* is "to follow your life-path and serve others". Your *Dharma* is your purpose and is synonymous with your Primary Mission.

In this context, I also quite like Deepak Chopra's definition, which says, *Dharma is your unique purpose in life [...] Everyone has a purpose in life – a unique gift or a special talent to benefit others. When you blend this talent with service to others, you experience the ecstasy and exultation of your own spirit, which is the objective.*

I am familiarizing you with the concept of *Dharma* because when you follow your *Dharma*, you experience continuous jubilation, deep contentment, and distinctive delight of an exceptionally high level which is difficult to put into words. This is the cardinal point here – you can learn about an idea or theme by reading and studying it, but that learning is at an intellectual level. However, when you experience an idea, the learning you achieve is in itself so much more potent and long-lasting.

I can say this confidently based primarily on my own experience and supported by the experiences of those I have worked with over the years. The feeling of fulfillment and exhilaration I experience when working on my enterprise and writing this book is indeed invaluable. Furthermore, because you are in spiritual harmony, it often feels that a force much bigger than you is taking your hand and guiding you to proceed on the path that you were always meant to take. The words "tiredness" or "fatigue" don't seem to feature in the vocabulary, and you feel energized in a way that appears divine.

It was one such day when I lost track of time working extremely late into the night, that I came across these words from the great Indian sage, Patanjali, who authored the *Yoga Sutras* – the very first Yoga work on which all others are based. Patanjali says:

When you're inspired by some great purpose, some extraordinary project, all your thoughts break their bonds. Your mind transcends limitations, your consciousness expands in every direction, and you find yourself in a new, great, and wonderful world. Dormant forces, faculties and talents become alive, and you discover yourself to be a greater person by far than you ever dreamed yourself to be.

I was absolutely besotted with these words that day and I continue to be even today. Patanjali didn't use the word *Dharma*, but his reference was exactly to following your *Dharma*.

Heart of the Matter

Follow your *Dharma*!

7.
BEING IN SPIRITUAL HARMONY: THE FIRST PREREQUISITE

7. BEING IN SPIRITUAL HARMONY: THE FIRST PREREQUISITE

He who lives in harmony with himself lives in harmony with the universe.

Marcus Aurelius

When you were introduced to the Multi-Pronged Model earlier, you learnt that there are three prerequisites associated with the kind of Primary Mission that enables you to manifest your infinite riches; the first of those is Being in Spiritual Harmony.

You are in spiritual harmony when what you want to manifest is fully aligned with the core values of your soul. The core values of your soul are: living Your Principal Mission, following the doctrine of "true creators are not competitors", and passing the Primary Vision test.

Each of the next three chapters is devoted to each of these core values. Before you review those core values, though, it is important you are acquainted with some terms and their definitions which might be new for you but will feature in the following chapters. These are:

Desire – This is the feeling of wanting to manifest a certain experience. All of us have multiple desires every few minutes. Some are whims, some are routine daily desires, yet some are pressing, meaningful desires that repetitively surface. The last category are authentic callings or the voice of your soul. These are the ones you must pay careful attention to and act on, and these are what we will concentrate on.

Universal Spirit – This is the all-encompassing energy that flows in and through everything and everyone. You can also think of it as the God substance, supreme intelligence, life source or, if you are a *Star Wars* fan, the Force.

Soul – Your soul is a fragment of universal spirit and the immortal essence of who you are. When you use everyday terms such as "your" body, "my" idea, etc., each of these pronouns refers to the soul. Think of the soul as synonymous with your spirit. James Cook said: *The soul is that part of you in harmony with God.*

Mind – Your mind is an intangible enterprise and not a tangible thing. Think of the mind most importantly as the bridge that connects your body to the soul, and thus to universal spirit.

Body – Your body is a mortal physical form that exists for the duration that your soul is on earth.

Brain – Contrary to what many people think, your brain is not your mind. Your brain is the most complex part of your body and based at the helm of your body… yet it is just another tangible organ in your body.

Heart of the Matter

Because your soul is a fragment of universal spirit, your being in spiritual harmony also means your desire works with the flow of universal spirit rather than against it. This directional flow further enhances the potency and speed of the manifestation experience.

8.
LIVING YOUR
PRIMARY MISSION

8. LIVING YOUR PRIMARY MISSION

The two most important days in your life are the day you are born and the day you find out why.

Mark Twain

Before you derive your Primary Mission, there are stages of understanding to take you through. Begin by thinking of your Primary Mission not as something separate from you – you should literally become your Primary Mission. The best way to understand this is through the ideas outlined in Thomas Troward's essay, *Entering into the spirit of it.*

Troward was one of the pioneering teachers of the New Thought Movement. While there are different views about who first used the term "Law of Attraction" in the context we understand it in contemporary times, Troward is one of the more probable people to have done so.

<u>Entering Into the Spirit of Your Primary Mission</u>

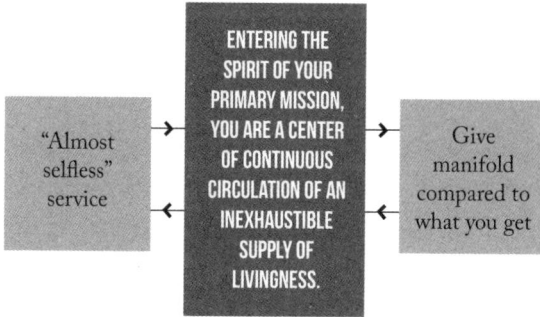

ENTERING THE SPIRIT OF YOUR PRIMARY MISSION, YOU ARE A CENTER OF CONTINUOUS CIRCULATION OF AN INEXHAUSTIBLE SUPPLY OF LIVINGNESS.

"Almost selfless" service → ← Give manifold compared to what you get

"Almost selfless" service means that your primary objective is to provide your services in the best possible manner for the betterment of those who use them. "Getting" is not the primary objective but an important side-effect.

As a **Center of Continuous Circulation**, you enter the spirit of your Primary Mission successfully and then set in motion the continuous circulation of your services, using the prosperity you generate in turn to elevate your services to the next level, and so on, in a never-ending cycle for the mutual betterment of all you interact with in the process.

Give manifold compared to what you get means your focus should be on living your Primary Mission, on what you give and how you serve others, rather than on what you get. Rest assured, you will get exactly what you want, but when your primary focus is on the giving and you treat the getting as an important side-effect, what you want will flock to you.

Over the years, while I've read through and reflected on many mission statements of global corporations, four stand out to me. They stand out to me because their incredible founders followed the concept of actually becoming and living the very missions they wrote about. These enterprises continue to flourish even today, and I would like to now share more about them with you.*

Apple Inc.: The most valuable company in the world with a market capitalization of $3.4 trillion. Steve Jobs' original mission statement was: *To make a contribution to the world by making tools for the mind that advance humankind.*

Ford Motor Company: When Henry Ford established the world's first mass market automobile/car company, his original mission was: *To build and market a simple, strong, reliable, affordable car for the masses;* this contrasted with the fact that in those days, owning an automobile was a luxury reserved only for the wealthy. As a farm boy himself, he specifically wanted to *help farm families become less isolated.* More than a hundred years

---

* Market capitalization figures are taken at different points between 2023 and 2024.

later, Ford Motor Company's market capitalization is about $50 billion.

Tata Group: JRD Tata, the scion of India's most valuable brand – valued at $28 billion and, arguably, the most valuable conglomerate with a market capitalization of more than $400 billion – lived by the mantra that: *No success or achievement in material terms is worthwhile, unless it serves the needs or interests of a country and its people and is achieved by fair and honest means.*

S.C. Johnson & Son Inc.: Owner of household brands such as Mr Muscle®, Kiwi®, Pledge®, and Baygon®, amongst many others, this business is still privately held and family-led despite annual revenue of more than $10 billion. A century ago, the second-generation family leader, Herbert Johnson Sr., summed up the philosophy of his enterprise as: *The goodwill of people is the only enduring thing in any business. It is the sole substance. The rest is shadow.* This guides the company even today.

Heart of the Matter

Living your Primary Mission is the first prerequisite of being in spiritual harmony. To live your Primary Mission means to literally become the mission yourself, embodying and displaying on a continuous basis what the mission stands for.

9.
TRUE CREATORS ARE
NOT COMPETITORS

9. TRUE CREATORS ARE NOT COMPETITORS

There is nothing noble in being superior to your fellow man; true nobility is being superior to your former self.

Ernest Hemingway

Following the first core value of your soul of living your Principal Mission, the next core value is your intention to create rather than compete. Unfortunately, a great deal of contemporary life is focused on the exploitation of natural talent for personal gain – to make the most of your own ability to beat others and to conquer all, to amass the most money, or acquire the largest mountain of material goods to reflect wealth, power, and success. And this is where the erroneous gap lies between competing rather than creating as the driving force. Like most people, you too will have often wondered whether there is enough for you and, perhaps, for others? As an example, if you wanted a promotion at work and there were two other people with the same desire, but only one of you got the promotion, you might ask, "How come? Isn't there supposed to be enough for us all?" Yes, you would be justified in asking this question, because from where you see this situation, there is not enough for all. My answer to this is:

"There is more than enough for you and for the rest of us, as long as you focus on Creation and not on Competition." An effective way to understand this better is through the understanding of the Different Levels of You, which not only helps you recognize the inherent values aligned with your Primary Mission at each level of the self, but also enables you to identify the level you should be at as you live your Primary Mission.

All human beings have four levels of awareness that co-exist, (Wayne Dyer in *Wishes Fulfilled* proposes a somewhat similar model explained in detail across a series of chapters). At any point in time, though, you are only operating on one of these levels.

The Different Levels of You

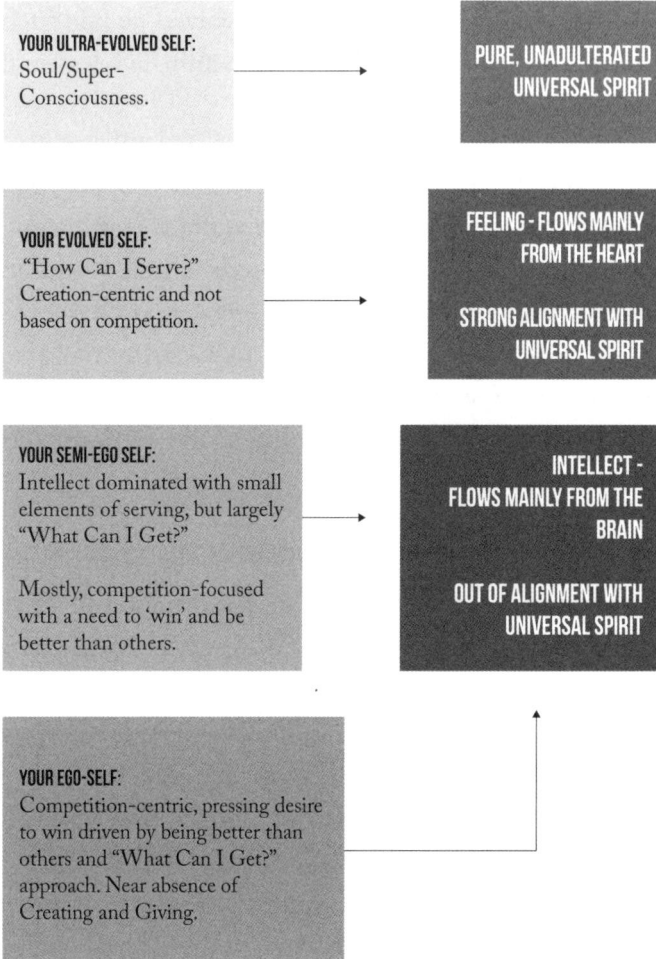

| YOUR ULTRA-EVOLVED SELF:
Soul/Super-
Consciousness. | → | PURE, UNADULTERATED
UNIVERSAL SPIRIT |

| YOUR EVOLVED SELF:
"How Can I Serve?"
Creation-centric and not
based on competition. | → | FEELING - FLOWS MAINLY
FROM THE HEART

STRONG ALIGNMENT WITH
UNIVERSAL SPIRIT |

| YOUR SEMI-EGO SELF:
Intellect dominated with small
elements of serving, but largely
"What Can I Get?"

Mostly, competition-focused
with a need to 'win' and be
better than others. | → | INTELLECT -
FLOWS MAINLY FROM THE
BRAIN

OUT OF ALIGNMENT WITH
UNIVERSAL SPIRIT |

YOUR EGO-SELF:
Competition-centric, pressing desire
to win driven by being better than
others and "What Can I Get?"
approach. Near absence of
Creating and Giving.

Your ultra-evolved self is your highest level of being and is synonymous with universal spirit. Messiahs such as Jesus, Buddha and Krishna mostly lived at and operated from this level, while other highly evolved people such as Mother Teresa and Mahatma Gandhi lived at and operated from just below this level.

Your evolved self is the next level and the one you should live at and operate from if you are manifesting your infinite riches. This is strongly aligned and in harmony with universal spirit. Moreover, at this level, you are living your Primary Mission, focusing most on what you can give and how you can serve others. You are beyond the competing phase and the predominant feeling is that of creating.

Now think about the missions of Steve Jobs, Henry Ford, JRD Tata and Herbert Johnson Sr., which you were introduced to in the last chapter. Ask yourself whether any of these missions has even the slightest feeling of trying to be better than others? Do these missions even touch upon competition in any manner? The answer is no, because the people behind these enterprises were singularly focused on providing a particular service, as evidenced in their mission statements – everything else worked around this primary purpose as they operated at the level of the evolved self.

The third level is your semi-ego self. This is mostly about the ego's need to win, be better than others, and compete.

The dominant objective is to get. There could be small elements of giving and creating, but mostly it is all about getting and winning, and is intellect-driven. This is where the majority of humankind operates from today. A typical mindset here would be one where the primary objective is about how much money can be made and how many sales closed in any year. There could well be a somewhat superficial mission lurking in the background supplemented with the perspective of the customer getting a product/service and, in the process, justifying that there is nothing wrong with focusing primarily on the money earned and sales closed.

The last level is your ego-self. This is as ego-centric as it gets and is entirely intellect-driven. The overarching objective is to compete, win and be better than others, and is as disassociated from universal spirit as can be. Think of this level as a more intense version of the semi-ego self. It is rare to operate in entirety from this place, but it is possible, and those who do would be a rather small minority.

Unfortunately, promoting competition has been a fundamental part of the mindset of most people, particularly in the global business community. This conditioning defines competing – or, more precisely, winning – as synonymous with progressing and developing. And "beating" another company or person is one of the most important tenets of many businesses.

In many ways, this is the foundation of the wider global ecosystem – **and is a foundational brick in the education system that distracts us from our Primary Mission.** All the way from school to university in the education system, in sport, entrepreneurship, and the corporate sector, humankind has taken itself to a state wherein the emphasis is typically on winning while competing, and not on creating while co-operating.

The Holy Grail then is the movement upwards from the semi-ego self to the evolved self. This is the change one needs to make as one aims to move away from living in the "ordinary" zone. Once you start to live in this new space, you prosper naturally, aligning with the *Spirit of Opulence* – something Troward articulates very well.

Another great work in this area, written about 80 years ago, is *Man's Search for Meaning,* which was Viktor Frankl's first book. The quotation that follows is from the introduction and naturally aligns with what you've been studying about your Primary Mission.

Don't aim at success. The more you aim at it and make it a target, the more you are going to miss it. For success, like happiness, cannot be pursued; it must ensue, and it only does so as the unintended side effect of one's personal dedication to a cause greater than oneself. Happiness must happen, and the same holds for success: you have to let it happen by not caring about it.

Heart of the Matter

Enterprises that thrive (not just survive) over time consciously or otherwise follow the maxim of true creators not being competitors.

10.
THE PRIMARY
VISION TEST

10. THE PRIMARY VISION TEST

Your Primary Vision is the physical form your Primary Mission takes.

Pushkar Anand

As the name suggests, the last core value is a Vision test. Unlike at the optician's, though, you will learn how to do this test yourself! Here is how you derive your Primary Vision.

The Four Tests

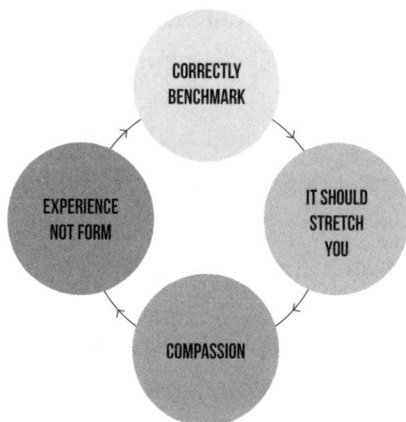

CORRECTLY BENCHMARK

IT SHOULD STRETCH YOU

COMPASSION

EXPERIENCE NOT FORM

To **correctly benchmark** translates into ensuring that the Vision targets creation and not competition, it contributes and gives in turn far more than what you receive, it positively impacts everyone you serve, and finally, the person you evolve into in the process takes precedence over what you receive.

Your Primary Vision should **stretch you** and make you feel at the outset that you need to reinvent yourself. Most importantly, you should currently not know how to get there.

While more than one personal development practitioner expounds this view, some six years ago, when I read Mike Dooley's *Playing the Matrix* and supplemented it with an online course of the same name, I loved how he talked about the Hows not being relevant. I still remember my favorite part when, on multiple occasions, he used the term "The Cursed Hows"! Cursed, because not knowing the "Hows" deters people quite easily from the destination they would ideally have liked – akin to the Primary Vision.

Your Primary Vision should operate with a foundation of **compassion**. Blaine Bartlett (Grandmaster B²) co-authored *Compassionate Capitalism: A Journey to the Soul of Business*, where he proposes exactly this idea.

Another valuable concept he has proposed is to **focus on the experience and not the form**. This leads to finding balance between the specific and the general. Too much specificity often contradicts correct benchmarking, while too little risks taking away focus.

You will now see two examples of contrasting Primary Visions. I am sharing these to help you develop your perspective as you work towards identifying your Primary Mission and Vision in the next chapter.

Primary Vision I

Compassionate CEO in the technology start-up sector by December 31, 2025, who develops new leaders and uses the power of technology to benefit the world.

This Vision passes the correctly benchmarking test because the focus is on creation rather than competition, with no mention of a particular corporation; there is clear mention of giving back while helping the wider ecosystem; and it appears to be transformative by developing people with the right leadership. It passes the second and third tests of stretching the person and being compassionate, respectively, because the objective is to be a CEO and, specifically, a compassionate CEO. Lastly, it passes the final test of focusing on the experience and not the form because it is somewhat specific yet directional, with the specificity coming from being CEO while not being overly specific focusing on a particular corporation.

Primary Vision II

A continuously-winning and ruthless CEO of company X by June 30, 2026.

This fails the first test to correctly benchmark because it focuses on competition and there is no mention of giving back or wider development. While it appears to pass the second pillar of stretching the person, considering the target is to become CEO, it fails the third test of being compassionate because not only is there an absence of compassion, it includes "continuously winning" and "ruthless", which are in complete opposition. Lastly, it fails the fourth pillar because it focuses on the form of being CEO of a specific company, rather than the experience.

On a related note, you should know that while on the one hand true creation happens in harmony with universal spirit, numerous not-very-nice and ruthless people are able to create voraciously as well. The fact is that when creation happens in disharmony with universal spirit, it comes with its baggage. Questions to consider here are whether such creation is sustainable, does it leave the creator and those impacted by that creation fundamentally happy, is it all about feeding the ego, and does it end badly?

The best example of this situation is from the start of Bob Proctor's *You Were Born Rich*, where he talks about a meeting in a US hotel of the eight wealthiest financiers, who collectively controlled more money than the US government. Twenty-five years later, each of them was either bankrupt or insane – or had committed suicide.

I am sharing this with you because I want you to know that while these men were all successful, wealthy and at the top of their game, somewhere along their respective journeys of empire-building and manifesting their goals, they lost the all-important gift of creating in harmony with universal spirit.

Having said that, all human beings have the gift of free will, and if there are those who feel that the path for them is to target creation when not in harmony with universal spirit, then that is their decision. They do possess the freedom to go down that path. However, anyone in harmony with the laws of nature and with universal spirit is unlikely to follow that path.

Heart of the Matter

Passing the Four Tests is critical for a Primary Vision that authentically corresponds to your Primary Mission and sits well within the framework of the Multi-Pronged Model.

11.
IDENTIFY YOUR PRIMARY MISSION & VISION

11. IDENTIFY YOUR PRIMARY MISSION & VISION

Your purpose in life is to find your purpose and give your whole heart and soul to it.

Buddha

Now that you are well-versed with the theory, it is time for you to start with the practical steps needed to unlock your infinite riches. On the one hand, you learnt that we all have a Primary Mission to fulfill, yet on the other you also learnt about the DR^3 Bubble, which often cuts us away from living our *Dharma* and fulfilling this mission. The first thing, then, is to help you re-connect with and identify your Primary Mission through the **Three-Step Re-connection Tool**™.

This tool comprises three steps to help you derive your Primary Mission and Vision. You need to devote three to four minutes to each step:

Exercise 1

Step 1: List between one and three of your biggest talents.

Step 2: List between one and three of your core values.

Step 3: If you had all that you wanted and there was no financial need to work, what would you like to do that would make you feel complete and energized? What is it that would result in a childish enthusiasm to share this great work with your nearest and dearest, with a twinkle in your eye? Write it down, also incorporating how, in the process, this can help those you would serve.

Once you have the answers, you then derive your Primary Mission and the corresponding Vision. Your Primary

Mission is a phrase or brief statement focused most on serving others. The corresponding Vision is a representation of what the Primary Mission successfully unfolding would look like... and yes, the important side-effect of financial abundance also features prominently!

The Primary Vision, and the side-effect of financial abundance, must be quantifiable and have specific timelines. To set you on your **Three-Step Re-connection Tool**™ journey, I am sharing three examples. The first is my own and the second is of a special client who has more than one Mission.

Centre for Infinite Riches®

Answers for Step I: Public speaking, writing, and inspiring others.

Answers for Step II: Expound the Mission with a Business and "Impression of Increase" way of life, stand for Compassionate Capitalism, and be a center for distributing infinite riches.

Answers for Step III: Uplift people, enabling them to live their Primary Mission or *Dharma* while manifesting their infinite riches.

Primary Mission: Uplift Humanity.

Primary Vision: Wake up four million people by enabling them to first identify and, then, manifest their infinite riches, and establish **Centre for Infinite Riches**® as a personal development brand known and respected across the world… by my 50th birthday on October 21, 2026.

Financial Abundance Side-Effect: My net worth is $X* by my 50th birthday on October 21, 2026.

Rowanvale Books

Cat Charlton – founder and Managing Director of Rowanvale Books – is not only my publisher globally (except in the Indian subcontinent) but also someone I have worked with closely in her personal development journey. Cat entered publishing when her father, who was keen to use a hybrid publisher, was deceived by more than one hybrid publisher and had a difficult experience trying to get his book in front of his audience. Her purpose was to ensure that every author she ever works with has a seamless experience and never has to endure what her father went through. You can read more about Cat and her journey on https://www.rowanvalebooks.com

---

* Figures are mostly not provided in the examples because of privacy reasons.

Like me, if you were to interact with Cat, you would observe that not only is she highly energetic but she also wants to do a lot of things! She is the only one I recommended to have more than one mission. Typically, I discourage multiple missions when they come up; the exception is in the odd case, where I feel this is best for the person and whom they serve.

Answers for Step I: Project Management and forging partnerships.

Answers for Step II: Honesty, fairness, and balance.

Answers for Step III: Empower others, especially those who need it most.

Principal Primary Mission: Empower authors, employees, and underprivileged entrepreneurs.

Primary Sub-Mission 1: Ensure authors have a seamless hybrid publishing experience.

Primary Sub-Mission 2: Pledge that every Rowanvale employee/freelancer has optimum work-life balance.

Primary Sub-Mission 3: Facilitate underprivileged entrepreneurs to develop their enterprises.

Principal Primary Vision: Rowanvale Books is recognized globally as: (i) A leading ethical hybrid publisher with brick-and-mortar distribution; (ii) A premier employer for enabling employees/freelancers to achieve optimum work-life balance; and (iii) An established mentor to aspiring underprivileged entrepreneurs… by April 11, 2027 – Cat's 37th birthday.

Primary Sub-Vision 1: Serve X authors to publish their books, including X bestsellers.

Primary Sub-Vision 2: All employees/freelancers totaling X have achieved optimum work-life balance.

Primary Sub-Vision 3: X underprivileged entrepreneurs have been positively impacted.

Financial Abundance Side-Effect: My net worth is $X by my 37th birthday on April 11, 2027.

Exercise 2

Drawing on the examples shared above, use the **Three-Step Re-connection Model**™ to draft your own Primary Mission and corresponding Vision. You will always have the freedom to adjust and improve your answers as you begin your journey. The answers do not have to be final at this stage, but it is important you have something drafted to proceed – else, you risk trying to perpetually improvise, and not make a start.

_____

_____

_____

_____

_____

_____

Heart of the Matter

Starting to identify your Primary Mission and Vision is a momentous landmark – well done!

12.
THE SCALE OF YOUR PRIMARY VISION

12. THE SCALE OF YOUR PRIMARY VISION

The greater the opportunity, the fewer are those who see it.

James Cook

When I first came across the last quotation by James Cook, it took me back twenty-five years when, as a recent graduate, I voraciously read Akio Morita's *Made in Japan*. Morita was the co-founder of the Sony Group Corporation and the driving force behind the enterprise. This book is autobiographical, more about Sony than about Morita.

In 1957, when Sony was an upcoming enterprise, it manufactured the world's first pocket-sized portable transistor radio, and for that received a massive order from the American company, Bulova Watch Company. However, Bulova's condition was that the radios be sold under the Bulova brand and not the Sony brand.

Morita's partner – the co-founder of Sony – as well as the senior leadership team, all thought Morita was crazy to refuse the deal and were keen to proceed with this arrangement; Morita, however, was adamant about not diluting the Sony brand and instead selling the radios branded as Sony. This became a rather contentious issue within Sony, but Morita eventually prevailed, convincing the others that Sony must stay true to its guiding principles, including adhering to its core mission or, in the context of what you have studied, its *Dharma*.

In the conversation that followed between Morita and the purchasing executive at Bulova, Morita was told he was missing a big opportunity and how futile it was to brand the radio as Sony, because no one knew Sony but everyone knew Bulova as an established brand of fifty years. Morita's reply was along the lines of, "Fifty years ago, no one knew Bulova; likewise, no one knows Sony today, but I am taking the first step today so that everyone will know about Sony in fifty years."

Today, Bulova is owned by the Japanese watchmaker, Citizen Watch Company, and of Citizen's annual revenue of about $2.2 billion, less than 10% comes from the Bulova brand. Sony today has annual revenue of about $88 billion.

Another example highlighting the same point is that of Wayne Dyer, as he writes in *Wishes Fulfilled*. Wayne shares the example of his bosses in the Navy telling him how, at the age of twenty-two, he was too old to start afresh and how his life would now be loaded with uncertainty. Wayne's thoughts were:

But I had a dream – an imagination filled with the idea of teaching, writing, and speaking to large audiences. I saw myself onstage. I saw myself as a prominent author. And this vision could not and would not be sabotaged by someone else's vision of what I should or could become.

Often when you set out defining your Primary Mission, while the mission in itself is valid, you determine its scale by your past experiences and conditioning. Most of the time, this would yield a mission, the scale of which is incrementally higher than the level you've been used to but is typically along what is called a linear path.

The Harvard-educated American academic, Albert Bartlett, recognized this and said:

The greatest shortcoming of the human race is our inability to understand the exponential function.

The main reason for this shortcoming is that society globally functions on the incremental-linear function – single digit growth figures are typically the norm. However, as you establish something new, then why stay linear and incremental? Instead, why not be radical and exponential?

Perhaps the best example to understand the concept of the exponential function is the Indian chess fable. The story goes that there was a minister who invented the game of chess and shared it with the king. The king, delighted with his work, asked him what he wanted in return. The minister humbly asked for a grain of rice for himself, double the quantity for his wife, double of that quantity for his mother, double of that for his father, and so on and so forth. Each family member – and then everyone in his village – was represented by a square on the chessboard, and the quantity kept doubling till they got to the last square on the board. This in turn translated into a final number equal to $(2)^{64}$ or about $(18$ billion$)^2$, which was many times more than the global wheat output! On the face of it, this looks like a small demand, and so the king thought too, but when the count started to increase after the first few squares, the extent of the magnification seemed to dawn on the king and he realized the scale of the demand…

Likewise, now see the scale of your enterprise from an exponential growth perspective. Even if you have historically targeted to grow, say, five percent or ten percent annually, if you get on the exponential growth bandwagon targeting, say, 150% growth in three years, the ask seems more achievable.

In the same vein, it is worth touching upon this concept of being reasonable and realistic. I often say that being reasonable and realistic yields reasonable and realistic results, while being unreasonable and unrealistic yields corresponding results! This does not mean that one should be unreasonable and unrealistic for the sake of being so. All it means is: do not constrain the calling you have from within because societal conditioning is to be reasonable and realistic.

Coincidentally, the great intellectual, George Bernard Shaw, also said:

The reasonable man adapts himself to the world: the unreasonable one persists in trying to adapt the world to himself. Therefore all progress depends on the unreasonable man.

Understanding and applying the thinking in this chapter will help you break away from the prevalent thinking of linear incremental progress and will further unshackle your ability to truly be free. This new thinking then profoundly develops your ability – especially when determining your Primary Vision – to set the scale of your impact to what you really want it to be rather than what you think you can achieve.

One beautiful thing about learning is that once you know how something can be achieved, half the journey is complete; the other half is successful implementation. Likewise, in this context, once you know the power of the exponential function, especially when compared with the linear one, you then have a solid foundation to ascend.

Accordingly, I find the **Rule of Three**™ a robust method, especially in the early part of one's journey.

Rule of Three™

> ➢ Use three-year timelines when setting your Primary Mission and Vision.

> ➢ Logically, and based on experience, whatever you think is the scale of your Primary Vision, increase it three times.

> ➢ Likewise, whatever you logically think can be your net worth, increase it three times.

Based on my experience over the years, increasing the scale of your Vision and net worth three times results in a good balance between starting to get stretched and "unreasonable and unrealistic", yet not taking it so far out that you lose sight of it altogether. Furthermore, what the **Rule of Three**™ does more as you commence your journey, is it helps you break away from your old way of thinking and puts you on the early steps of the ladder of somewhat unreasonable thinking. The reason for the three-year timeline is that it is neither imminent like a one-year perspective nor is it as far out as ten years; as you start to walk on this path, it puts you in a strong position to be exponential yet selectively keep the best parts of the incremental approach. As you develop further on this path, you evolve to be even more exponential, while keeping the doors open to choose the odd tool from the incremental approach to supplement the exponential mindset.

Lastly, don't lose sight of the fact that you have twenty-four hours in the day, irrespective of the scale of your Vision. Whether you aim high or low, whether you decide to reach for the stars or otherwise, there is only that much time you have each day to make the impact you want to.

Napoleon Hill made a similar point, almost a century ago:

No more effort is needed to aim high in life, to demand abundance and prosperity, than is required to accept misery and poverty.

Exercise 1

With what you've learnt in this chapter, think about the renewed scale of your Primary Vision and Financial Abundance Side-Effect, which you drafted through Exercise 2 in the last chapter; now scale them upwards accordingly.

_____

_____

_____

_____

_____

_____

Heart of the Matter

Stop being incremental, realistic, and reasonable – start being radical, unrealistic, and unreasonable with your dreams!

13.
MONEY, MONEY, MONEY: IS IT REALLY ABOUT THE MONEY?

13. MONEY, MONEY, MONEY: IS IT REALLY ABOUT THE MONEY?

I let money serve its purpose, but I don't live to serve money. I think that is why we have such a beautiful relationship.

Oprah Winfrey

In the opening chapter in Part I, you read that:

> *There is a subsequent chapter titled* **Money, Money, Money: Is It Really About The Money?** *where you will learn all about* **The Six Statutes of Money**™.

> *At this point however, I would like you to have some context on the role of money to carry forward with you as you read through this book, and so, giving you a sneak peek, I am introducing you to one of these Statutes,* **The Rules of Receiving Money**.

This is exactly why this chapter has been written and placed at the point just after you have drafted your Primary Mission, Vision, and Financial Abundance Side-Effect – so that you can slot money in its rightful place and let it serve its purpose without distracting you from living your Primary Mission.

The Six Statutes of Money™

1. Unlearn what you have historically learnt about your relationship with money.	2. Decide exactly how much money to your name will ensure that you will not need to think about a lack of money ever again.
3. Nothing is **BIG** or small as an absolute – you give that label.	4. There is one difference between people with more money than they need and you, and you can overcome this with the right study and discipline.
5. Money in itself is worth nothing but is valuable because of what it represents.	6. The Rules of Receiving Money.

Statute I – Unlearn what you have historically learnt about your relationship with money.

Exercise 1

Write down, in two or three lines each, what your current relationship with money is and – more importantly, going forward – what you would like it to be. Questions you can ask yourself, but are not restricted to, are:

(i)   Do I control money, or does money control me?

_____

_____

(ii) Is money my master, or am I money's master?

_____

_____

(iii) Does working longer hours lead to me getting more money?

_____

_____

(iv) Other than working harder, is there anything I can do to get the amount of money I truly desire?

_____

_____

Statute II – Decide exactly how much money to your name will ensure that you will not need to think about a lack of money ever again.

This Statute is as simple as it gets – what would you like your net worth to be? Do not be concerned with how you will obtain this net worth – if at this stage you start to think about the *Cursed Hows* you learnt about earlier, you will not be able to determine what you truly want your net worth to be. Admit to yourself what you truly want your net worth to be – forget about the *how* at this point!

Exercise 2

Ignoring the *how,* and without putting a timeline to achieve this net worth, write down what you would like your net worth to be.

Statute III – Nothing is BIG or small as an absolute – you give that label.

At first, this might sound absurd to you. I say so because when I came across this concept the first time, I thought so too. However, as I studied and enhanced my awareness over time, I learnt not only is this true, but it is also one of the most valuable ideas to embrace.

There is a simple metaphor I find most useful to reinforce this point. It takes two extreme cases, but these are needed to help you appreciate this statute.

Assume there is a mega-project, which the world's wealthiest person is eager to invest in. To participate, the funding needed from this person is $220 billion but their net worth is "merely" $200 billion. The world's wealthiest person is therefore not wealthy enough to fund this project their heart is really set on. Suddenly, their net worth is not **BIG** but small when seen in this context.

Separately, assume there is a person who spends their time as a recluse living in a little hut up in the mountains with a small plot of land where they farm fruit and vegetables, partially for their own consumption and partially to earn a living. Their net worth is $3,000 and the supporting income is just enough to finance three meals a day and the basic utilities of this little hut. This person's requirement, though, is two meals a day, thus leaving them with a surplus cash-flow on an ongoing basis. Suddenly, with a net worth of $3,000 and a basic farming venture, the money they have is **BIG** and not small.

You see now – nothing is **BIG** or small as an absolute because you give that label!

Statute IV – There is one difference between people with more money than they need and you, and you can overcome this with the right study and discipline.

Irrespective of whether they are consciously aware of it or not, or whatever name they give their model of financial success, people with more money than they need successfully execute the learnings of the **Multi-Pronged Model** you were introduced to. Once you master this model and, more importantly, the ability to successfully apply its key learnings, you too will be on your way to joining those who have more money than they need.

Statute V – Money in itself is worth nothing but is valuable because of what it represents.

Money as a standalone commodity is not worth the paper it is printed on!

Of all features of money, the **most powerful** is that it gives you **freedom of time**. Remember that *even the wealthiest person in the world has only twenty-four hours in a day.* Now, imagine a life wherein you have complete freedom of time because you do not need to worry about generating that income, for which you have been toiling all day.

Exercise 3

Assuming you have freedom of time and all the money you want, write a brief description of your ideal life. Feel free to write as you please, but I have often found that some specific descriptors are valuable. These include, most importantly, what you would do to keep yourself occupied, the kind of home you would like to live in, how you would contribute to society, and how you would entertain yourself. Try to keep this description to four or five lines.

Statute VI – The Rules of Receiving Money.

The Statute, *The Rules of Receiving Money*, says that the money you receive directly relates to:

(i) Whether the dominant sentiment of your enterprise is to "Give" an exceptional product/service experience or to "Get" the maximum amount of money.

(ii) Your purpose, and whether your enterprise adequately represents that purpose.

_____

_____

(iii) What is unique or truly special about your enterprise.

_____

_____

Exercise 4

Answer the three questions above for your enterprise.

I should add that Bob Proctor's _Law of Compensation_ is the only time I've come across anyone else attempting to answer why you receive a certain amount of money in exchange for what your enterprise provides. It says that the amount of money you earn will always be in exact ratio to: (1) The need for what you do; (2) Your ability to do it; and (3) The difficulty there will be in replacing you.

PART II

Exercise 5

Now, ask yourself whether you think it is about the money or not, and how you feel about Oprah Winfrey's quotation at the start of this chapter. As you write down your answer, consider these factors:

(i) Would having this much money contradict me authentically living my Primary Mission or *Dharma*? (ii) Will I not be able to focus on serving others if I have this amount of money? (iii) How can I do my job or run my enterprise successfully if generating money for myself is not the key objective? (iv) I love money! Why should I not make it about the money? What about the example of the eight wealthiest people, in Chapter 10?

When I thought through these questions, I realized that:

- ❖ While it was not about the money for me, I did want a certain amount of money.

- ❖ While the Primary Mission towers above the money focus as the central target, money is an important side-effect of living my Primary Mission.

❖ I zoned in on **The Rules of Receiving Money** because if you score highly on its three rules then you will not need to think about the money. This is because following these rules will take care of the abundant flow of money.

Once I got this far, for my benefit, I summarized my answer which, now, for your benefit, I am sharing with you:

It is NOT about the money BUT you cannot ignore the money. Focus on living your Primary Mission and write down what you want your Financial Abundance Side-Effect figure to be. Beyond that, do NOT focus on the money but on serving others, significantly enriching their lives, and getting better and better at what you do – the money will keep coming and coming.

Heart of the Matter

Read this chapter again. As you proceed on the path to manifesting your infinite riches, continue to refer back to and/or adapt the answers to the exercises in this chapter. Do that periodically until you feel 100% comfortable with the new relationship you've forged with money!

14.

MANAGE THE SUBCONSCIOUS: THE SECOND PREREQUISITE

14. MANAGE THE SUBCONSCIOUS: THE SECOND PREREQUISITE

Everything in this world is created twice – first in thought, then in form.

Mary Morrissey

Mary Morrissey has been a personal development teacher for more than four decades. As an eighteen-year-old and mother of an infant in the late 1960s, Mary was diagnosed with a fatal kidney disease and given six months to live.

The night before her operation, as was the norm, the hospital chaplain came to visit her. As they spoke, the chaplain told her that everything is created twice, and while everyone knows this, hardly anyone knows the power of knowing this! Before things are things, they are thoughts. As examples, she pointed out the bed, curtains, and the gown Mary was wearing. She then asked Mary what she would really like to do if she lived, and Mary replied that she would love to raise her boy with a lot of love and be a teacher. The chaplain further discussed with Mary that she could heal in entirety if she saw herself in good health but, most importantly, if she let go of the resentment she felt for herself. Sadly, Mary did feel rather resentful towards herself because when her school discovered her pregnancy, she was shamed and transferred to a different school for delinquent boys and pregnant girls.

To cut a long story short, Mary had her operation, changed her thinking by altering what she felt for herself within based on what the chaplain said, and four months later, when the doctors reviewed her case, their words were: *"We have no science for why your one kidney that was fifty percent destroyed is operating as a fully functioning kidney now. Whatever you've been doing, keep doing it."* Mary is in her seventy-fifth year now.

Your outer world is just a mirror of your inner world; as *The Kybalion* says: *As above so below; as below, so above.*

This is further reinforced in another personal development classic, *As a Man Thinketh*:

Mind is the Master power that molds and makes, And Man is Mind, and evermore he takes The tool of Thought, and, shaping what he wills, Brings forth a thousand joys, a thousand ills: — He thinks in secret, and it comes to pass: Environment is but his looking-glass.

Alternatively, **whatever** exists within you reflects outwards in physical form. The **whatever** within you is known as a "pattern" and it rests in your subconscious mind, which you will learn all about in the next chapter.

Moreover, depending on whose work you are studying, terms often used interchangeably with "patterns" in the subconscious mind are programs, beliefs, habits, auto-pilot mode, etc. Bob Proctor, in particular, used the term "paradigms".

Let's now look at the example of learning to ride a bicycle. To the untrained eye, riding a bicycle is about using your hands, legs, and the rest of your body in a certain manner. Yes, that is correct, but it is only the outward manifestation of an internal process. These parts of your body and your body itself are just the apparatus in action. Behind this apparatus, there is a powerful resource that gives the apparatus direction such that it can function in a cohesive manner. This force, invisible in the daily scheme of things, is the mind, and the direction it gives is the pattern that has been established within the mind.

In this example, the pattern that exists in your mind is the one of you successfully riding a bicycle. Based on this pattern, the body – which is the apparatus linked to the mind – takes the necessary action, and you experience the physical manifestation of successfully riding the bicycle. Even if you haven't ridden a bicycle for the last twenty years, once you get on it, the pattern will take over and your body will take the necessary action for you to succeed.

Another example is multiplication tables. Whether you like math or not, if asked, you will easily be able to recite basic tables such as two or three, even if you have not said them aloud in years. The reason here, as well, is that the pattern has been well-established since childhood, and when you want to say these tables aloud or even just to yourself, the brain and rest of the body apparatus act under the direction of the mind.

Patterns have always existed for every manifestation experienced in your life. The nucleus of this book is about you manifesting your infinite riches and so the material here will stay focused on the pattern(s) aligned with manifesting your infinite riches.

Now that you have developed an initial understanding of patterns, I would like you to note that if you want to achieve a certain manifestation, then you need to instill the matching pattern within you.

This is simple, but not easy – we touched upon this analogy earlier but will go into a little more depth now. Simplicity is the absence of complexity, while ease is the absence of disciplined effort and study to get the result you want. For example, if you are thirsty, you drink water – this is a simple concept. However, turning the tap and filling your glass is easy for an adult, but not easy for a child who is not tall enough to operate a tap and put the glass under the running water. Likewise, instilling a new pattern is a simple concept, but before it becomes an easy concept, you must master the steps needed to do so.

Heart of the Matter

Consciously managing the subconscious mind requires focused work and following specific steps – you will learn these in the next two chapters.

15.
FUNDAMENTAL
CONCEPTS

15. FUNDAMENTAL CONCEPTS

The best and most beautiful things in the world cannot be seen or even touched – they must be felt with the heart.

Helen Keller

You were introduced to the subconscious mind in the previous chapter, and you will learn how best to manage it in the next chapter, and beyond. However, to fully appreciate the pages that follow, you must be familiar with some fundamental concepts first.

Fundamental Concept 1: The Mind

Your mind is the best and most beautiful thing you have. Most people struggle to define the mind, and some even treat it as synonymous with the brain. Invisible to the eye, think of the mind as an intangible enterprise, not a tangible thing. The brain, on the other hand, is a tangible, physical organ. The body and all its individual parts work cohesively with the brain at the helm, under the guidance of the mind. Of course, the brain is the most complex and paramount organ of the body, and techniques such as meditation and concepts such as neuroplasticity go a long way in making the brain more aligned with what you want to achieve. Nevertheless, if you think of the brain as the CEO, then think of the mind as the Chairman – the boss of the CEO!

A simple example to better appreciate the mind-brain difference is when you read about people in hospital who have been in a coma or "brain-dead" but, when they come back to their natural state, recall that in the comatose state they had awareness of all that was going on. That awareness comes from the mind, which goes beyond the physical faculties. Likewise, as is commonly known, animals have less-developed brains than humans but more evolved instincts; those evolved instincts also come directly from the mind. If you want to learn more, I recommend the work of the neuroscientist, Dr. Caroline Leaf.

The mind comprises the conscious mind and the subconscious mind. The subconscious mind is much more powerful than the conscious mind and is best thought of as the power center of the mind. The conscious mind accounts for less than ten percent of mind power, and the subconscious for more than ninety percent. If you would like to learn more about the mind, I would suggest Joseph Murphy's *The Power of Your Subconscious Mind*, first published in 1963 and widely regarded as the most influential book on the mind.

The conscious mind is the intellectual or thinking part of the mind and can swiftly accept or reject information and ideas. The five physical senses – See, Smell, Taste, Touch and Hear – are the faculties through which the conscious mind is acquainted with ideas and information.

The subconscious mind, on the other hand, is the feeling or emotional part of the mind and cannot reject what permeates through to it. It receives ideas and information exclusively through the conscious mind and, unlike the conscious mind (which can accept or reject swiftly), needs consistent repetition for the ideas or information to enter. Because it cannot reject, what it eventually accepts it treats as true, instilling the relevant pattern. Negatives (or the word "not") do not exist in this realm. So, if you say to yourself or think/feel that, for example, you have no ill health or no debt, the subconscious mind will see it as you having ill health or debt. By contrast, if you say or think/feel that you have perfect health or abundant wealth, the subconscious will consider you healthy or wealthy. **Furthermore, the subconscious mind cannot tell the difference between what is imagined as true and what is real in a physical sense – what it considers true, whether imagined or**

physically there, it converts into a pattern and the equivalent manifests in your life.

The simple diagram below shows the key features of both the conscious and subconscious minds, while also showing that you can reach the subconscious mind only through the conscious mind.

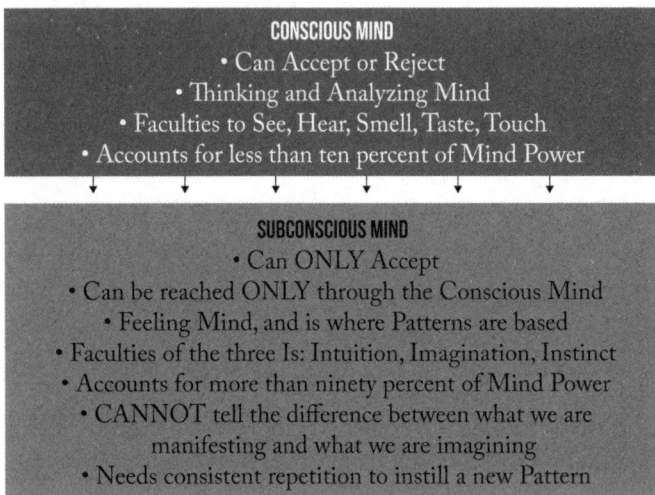

CONSCIOUS MIND
- Can Accept or Reject
- Thinking and Analyzing Mind
- Faculties to See, Hear, Smell, Taste, Touch
- Accounts for less than ten percent of Mind Power

SUBCONSCIOUS MIND
- Can ONLY Accept
- Can be reached ONLY through the Conscious Mind
- Feeling Mind, and is where Patterns are based
- Faculties of the three Is: Intuition, Imagination, Instinct
- Accounts for more than ninety percent of Mind Power
- CANNOT tell the difference between what we are manifesting and what we are imagining
- Needs consistent repetition to instill a new Pattern

Fundamental Concept 2: The Law of Vibration and the Law of Attraction

Everything is energy and that's all there is to it. Match the frequency of the reality you want, and you cannot help but get that reality. It can be no other way. This is not philosophy. This is physics.

Darryl Anka

You learnt earlier that universal spirit is present in everything and everyone – this is also what comprises atoms. Remember your basic chemistry lesson at school? Everything and everyone are made of atoms, which are in a perpetual state of motion – this is what lies behind all things and people. Because everything is energy, and energy is neither created nor destroyed and is never still, everything is in a constant state of movement. This state of movement is referred to as vibration and is measured in frequencies.

Michael Beckwith summarizes it well:

We are vibrational beings. […] If you put anything under a microscope, an intense microscope, you can ultimately see that everything is vibration. […] And when we lift our vibration to what we want to experience, it happens first on a vibratory level. And then it shows up and manifests in our life.

The revered book, *The Kybalion*, makes the same point:

Nothing rests; everything moves; everything vibrates.

The Law of Attraction is a popular term in everyday usage but is a secondary law which follows the primary law – the Law of Vibration. This is because the Law of Attraction is about attracting what you are in harmony with. However, you are in harmony with what is on the same vibration as you are on. In other words, you attract what is vibrating at the same rate as you are. Isn't it natural, then, that the Law of Vibration is primary?

By way of an example, say, while driving, you change the radio channels in the car. Each time you do, by the inherent nature of the matching frequency, you manifest the contents of that channel. Now, think of patterns as vibrations measured in human frequencies and, like the radio, you will see that you manifest physically the experience that corresponds to your frequency. Of course, there are innumerable patterns, but only one that corresponds to any specific manifestation experience.

Furthermore, the fact that everything vibrates is as applicable to a rock as it is to a sofa and, most importantly, to you. While a rock and a sofa vibrate too, they vibrate at relatively basic levels and are unable to manifest any experiences into their lives. A dog, meanwhile, vibrates at a relatively higher level compared to a rock or a sofa, and can manifest experiences such as food or a walk. Human beings are nature's most advanced embodiment and have the capability to vibrate and, consequently, manifest at much higher levels than all other embodiments of nature.

Fundamental Concept 3: The Subconscious Mind-Manifestation Linkage

As you now know, patterns in the subconscious mind account for the entire set of experiences you manifest in your life.

Nonetheless, there is no existing method to identify your patterns because humankind has not evolved to such a level. However, the manifestation results in your life are a direct reflection of the matching patterns within your subconscious. Consequently, the best approach to then manifest your desire is to work backwards and instill the corresponding pattern mirroring your desire.

For example, if you receive $40,000 a year, then we know that your corresponding pattern is $40,000 a year. Now, let's say that you want it to be $250,000 instead. This way, you know the new pattern to instill into the subconscious mind is that of you receiving $250,000.

A pattern can only be established in the subconscious mind through the conscious mind – there is no other route to do so! So, for a new pattern to be instilled in the subconscious mind, not only does it first need to progress from the conscious mind into the subconscious, but then it also needs to successfully replace the existing pattern prevalent in the subconscious.

Even if the new pattern of $250,000 has entered the subconscious mind, you will continue to receive $40,000 a year until it has entirely replaced the existing $40,000 pattern. In all cases, there will be a time when there is a tug of war between the two patterns, and both are simultaneously prevalent during this interim period. This will yield results that are a combination of the two. The exact result at any point in time will depend on the extent of the advantage or upper hand that a particular pattern has. If, in the given example, you are in a situation whereby the two patterns are equally matched, then you will receive the mid-point sum ($40,000/2 + $250,000/2 = $145,000).

Rest assured, there will be an intense battle between the two patterns before one emerges as the clear winner. Alternatively, there may not be a clear winner, and you'll end up somewhere in the spectrum between the two warring factions. This will obviously translate into results somewhere along the spectrum as well.

The reason for the stubbornness of the original patterns is that these have been in place for years, if not decades, and you have created them subconsciously without really knowing what was going on. On the contrary, we are now consciously trying to replace them and so need to learn new methods to do so. These methods, although simple and straightforward, will not yield results overnight because of the historical strength of the old patterns. These are time-tested, though, and will certainly yield the manifestation results if you follow them in a disciplined manner on an ongoing basis.

Fundamental Concept 4: The Soul-Desire Linkage

When you feel a pressing desire, you must take notice because that desire is a calling emanating from your soul. A straightforward rule of nature is that if you have a genuine desire, then not only has it come from your soul, but the means to achieve it are also there. Most probably, you will neither know the means nor have the skills initially, and there will be specific action steps that you will need to take. Nevertheless, unless the inherent ability to achieve it is there, the desire would not emanate. **This is a simple idea but a radically different one from the norm you might be used to.** Jack Canfield made the same point in somewhat different words: *You are not given a dream unless you have the capacity to fulfill it.*

Heart of the Matter

The fundamental concepts from this chapter, when studied in tandem with one another, substantially elevate your comprehension of instilling new patterns. The power of this information is magnified when studied alongside the contents of the next chapter.

16.
THE TEN PHASES TO INSTILL THE PERFECT PATTERN™

16. THE TEN PHASES TO INSTILL THE PERFECT PATTERN™

I did then what I knew how to do. Now that I know better, I do better.

Maya Angelou

A few years ago, during my journey of learning, I devoted a weekend solely to writing down the **Ten Phases to Instill the Perfect Pattern**™. At that point, I did it to consolidate my own understanding of the subject. The Ten Phases that follow are a refined version of the output of that weekend, and I know that they will consolidate your understanding too.

1. Any pressing desire we feel is initially felt in the conscious mind and has emanated from the soul.

2. The conscious mind can swiftly accept or reject the desire; if it rejects, then that ends the manifestation process for that desire.

3. If the conscious mind accepts the desire, then targeted work is needed to instill the desire into the subconscious mind. Unlike the conscious mind, the subconscious mind needs to be worked upon through repetition before the new desire feeds through. Consequently, the desire needs to be repeated on an ongoing basis before it feeds through from the conscious mind into the subconscious mind.

4. Once the desire enters the subconscious mind, a significant step has been achieved. This desire then establishes a new pattern in the subconscious mind. Think of this pattern, though, as a "start-up" pattern at this stage.

5. However, this fledgling pattern is not strong enough to reflect a manifestation. This is because there will be an existing pattern corresponding to the old version of that desire already in the subconscious.

6. There will now be a tug of war between the new pattern and the historically-established old pattern.

7. This is when heightened focus and targeted work is required to give all the ammunition needed for the new pattern to prevail and replace the historically-established pattern.

8. If the new pattern is unable to prevail in the tug of war, then the historically-established pattern continues – you are on the same vibration, and your body will take the same old actions for you to see the same old manifestation.

9. If the two patterns are evenly matched in the tug of war, then your body will take both old and new actions. This will cause you to see results that are somewhere between the old and new patterns. Another way of saying this is that there is a partial manifestation.

10. When the new pattern prevails in the tug of war, it then replaces in entirety the historically-established pattern. The body then takes corresponding new action, and you experience the new manifestation.

The information you have accessed in this chapter and the previous one is invaluable. Nonetheless, there is one final ingredient needed for you to complete the picture, and that is to see yourself as already having become the person you want to be. In other words, the frequencies of your Primary Vision and Financial Abundance Side-Effect should reflect your Primary Vision and Financial Abundance Side-Effect as already manifested!

Let me help you develop this idea further.

As you have learnt, you manifest physically the equivalent of the vibrational frequency of the prevalent pattern in the subconscious, which cannot tell the difference between what is true and what it falsely believes to be true. Let's now take a look at an example.

Like the rest of us, at some point you will have observed an exceptional actor performing locally in a small-time production and just about getting by while, on the other hand, you will have observed an average actor achieve star status on the big screen. The reason for this apparent paradox is the vibrational frequency of the actors' respective patterns; the manifestation result is nothing but a reflection of what is going on inside. In this example, the average actor has a pattern that they are exceptional, while the great actor's pattern is that they are just about average.

Seeing this through a slightly different lens, you will notice that because the subconscious mind – through a pattern – assumes that something is true, irrespective of whether it physically is or not, the most potent method to instill the perfect pattern – or to be on that frequency – is for the subconscious mind to treat your desire as already manifested. Conversely, if you instill the pattern that you "want" something, then will the manifestation not be one where you continue to chase what you want... so it remains a want?

This is such an elementary principle, yet truly understood by few people. This is also a radical shift in approach for anyone who starts to study this subject because until you were introduced to this material, the "normal" method of approaching a desire from a feeling perspective was moving towards realizing it. On the contrary, I am asking you now from a feeling perspective to assume that the desire has already manifested for you.

There are multiple methods you can use to ensure your pattern is one that assumes you already have what you desire, and you will shortly be introduced to many of these.

Heart of the Matter

See yourself as already having become the person you want to be.

17.
ONGOING GUIDED ACTION: THE THIRD PREREQUISITE

17. ONGOING GUIDED ACTION: THE THIRD PREREQUISITE

*Everything you want is out there waiting for you to ask.
Everything you want also wants you. But you have to take
action to get it.*

Jack Canfield

One consistent feature of most people's lives is that they'll take action to fulfill any desire they have. I say "most" and not "all" people, because there is a tiny number of people in the world who are at such a high level of awareness, living at and operating from their ultra-evolved selves, that they can instantly manifest. Whether we call their level Christ-consciousness, enlightenment, liberation, or something else, is secondary; what matters is that all the rest of us must take action to manifest. The irony is that these highly-evolved beings have negligible worldly needs, making it highly unlikely that manifesting would be of much interest to them!

Ongoing Guided Action is defined as action you take specifically to manifest your infinite riches. Think of it as the action needed to given them physical form.

What you must appreciate is that Ongoing Guided Action is not the same as the action you have historically been taking every day – that is daily action needed to physically get through the day. Rest assured, that has its own place and is a relevant contributor to living your life. However, if you think of your days in the DR^3 Bubble, or if you can think of others who have been there, you will recall that most of the actions that take place there are not in the category of Ongoing Guided Action.

Conversely, think of people you know who have manifested their infinite riches, and you will see that a significant proportion of the action they take is in the Ongoing Guided Action category.

In hindsight, when I think of all the mentors I've had over the last twenty-five years at different stages of my journey (each of whom has been rather successful in their own right), the common thread binding them all has been their ability to shut out the noise and focus most on "doing what really matters". Doing what really matters is another phrase for Ongoing Guided Action.

Now that you have a good idea of the core concept at play here, let's delve more into how this can propel you to manifest your infinite riches. An important thing for you to know more about here is the link between the desired frequency and Ongoing Guided Action.

Once you start to use the manifestation methods you will study in Part III and are in harmony with universal spirit, as the new pattern starts to take shape in the subconscious mind, you are then partially on the required frequency. At this point, in addition to using the manifestation methods, specific action is needed to further strengthen the new pattern, which is in its formative stages.

As you go through the process, by virtue of partially being on the required frequency, you will receive inspiration, impulses, or guidance to take specific action. Do NOT ignore these; instead, prioritize them and act on them as soon as you can. Universal spirit loves speed and communicates with you through this guidance. When you listen to the guidance and act accordingly, you are then taking Ongoing Guided Action and doing exactly what you need to at this point in the journey.

At times, this guidance will appear logical and as expected while, at other times, it will be unexpected and possibly somewhat illogical. Do not let that get in your way. The reason for it appearing illogical is that you judge it based on your intellect, which is informed by past events and is, by virtue of its inherent nature, limited in its perspective. On the contrary, you are receiving guidance from universal spirit, which is all encompassing. It has a plan for you, which you are not expected to question or doubt, but just have the faith and go along.

The best example that comes to my mind here is the role of Jack Canfield in spreading the message of the very book you are reading.

You will recall I said in the Introduction that some books are constant companions we must re-visit on a regular basis. One such book for me is *Chicken Soup for the Soul*. Because it is a collection of brief stories, I mostly read one or two stories each time.

I vividly remember it was a wet, dark and cold February evening in London when I picked up my copy of *Chicken Soup for the Soul* on an impulse. I'd decided a few minutes before to read another book, but the pull to read *Chicken Soup for the Soul* at that moment was unusually strong and I went with the flow. Within a few seconds, my gaze went to the section on *Live Your Dream*, and within that to the story titled *Follow Your Dream* by Jack Canfield.

This is a rather short story that took me a couple of minutes to read, but I will never forget the moment as I was reaching the end of the story. I had tears in my eyes and a lump in my throat due to a dreamlike inspiration that flashed through my mind, and the emotion was magnified by not only the inspiration but also the conviction that I was on the right path. My intellect can never justify that conviction; you see, it came from universal spirit and not from the intellect!

The inspiration, in turn, was that Jack was delighted with the message of this book and was playing an important part helping spread its message to a large number of people across the world. It is a different matter that I had no idea whatsoever how I would get in front of Jack, and whether he would even like to play a part! Practicing diligently what I have advocated in this chapter and taking encouragement from one of Jack's quotations that you read on Page 103 (*You are not given a dream unless you have the capacity to fulfill it*), I continued on this path and let the dream manifest as it was meant to...

What happens when you do as I did, is that you help the new pattern get stronger and progress more on that frequency. This is also the stage when the new pattern starts to gain the upper hand in the tug of war. You must continue to take Ongoing Guided Action and wait for further guidance. When you receive further guidance, which will almost always come to you as an impulse or hunch to take the next step, then do so. This cycle of using manifestation methods to consolidate the pattern, receiving guidance, taking Ongoing Guided Action based on that guidance, strengthening the pattern further, and the cycle continuing until you manifest, is indeed the last concept you need to know before progressing to Part III.

Heart of the Matter

Ongoing Guided Action must be undertaken day in, day out as you work to manifest your infinite riches.

PART III

→

SET IN MOTION YOUR INFINITE RICHES

←

18.
GET ON *THAT* FREQUENCY: AN INITIAL OVERVIEW

18. GET ON *THAT* FREQUENCY: AN INITIAL OVERVIEW

Assume the feeling of the wish fulfilled…

Neville Goddard

Of the three prerequisites, the one that needs most work and focus is Managing the Subconscious. Unlike Being in Spiritual Harmony – which directly translates into your Primary Mission – and Ongoing Guided Action – which becomes a part of your life – a new pattern needs relentless repetition and disciplined work to replace the one already there.

As you previously learnt, the existing pattern has been there for many years, if not decades, and this is what makes it stubborn. Moreover, because there is no known method to identify a prevalent pattern in the subconscious mind other than working backwards based on your manifestation results, the importance of your focus, dedication, and discipline is even more relevant.

What follows below is what you read earlier on Page 108-109, Chapter 16 in Part II; do read it once more.

...because the subconscious mind – through a pattern – assumes that something is true, irrespective of whether it physically is or not, the most potent method to instill the perfect pattern – or to be on that frequency – is for the subconscious mind to treat your desire as already manifested. Conversely, if you instill the pattern that you "want" something, then will the manifestation not be one where you continue to chase what you want... so it remains a want?

This is such an elementary principle, yet truly understood by few people. This is also a radical shift in approach for anyone who starts to study this subject because until you were introduced to this material, the "normal" method of approaching a desire from a feeling perspective was moving towards realizing it. On the contrary, I am asking you now from a feeling perspective to assume that the desire has already manifested for you.

There are multiple methods you can use to ensure your pattern is one that assumes you already have what you desire, and you will shortly be introduced to many of these.

Considering human beings are all inherently the same, yet different in their approaches to life, which methods work best for you is determined by what feels most natural to you. What works well for one person might not work that effectively for another. You will need to see what feels right for you by trying different methods to decide which is your best combination – combination, because you will often experience a stronger manifestation when it is approached from multiple sides rather than just one.

I will now introduce you to a marvelous law of nature called the Law of Cause and Effect, which says that a specific cause leads to a specific corresponding effect. The most spectacular feature of this law is its corollary, which is hardly ever written about. The corollary is that if a certain effect has manifested, then a corresponding cause led to that manifestation.

Let's take this further with a basic everyday example. You would agree that when you drink water, you get a specific feeling of satisfaction that comes only from drinking water. If you reverse this, then is it not natural to say when you have this very feeling, it means you have drunk water?

Reversing the analogy was first suggested by a great mystic of the 20th century. Wayne Dyer often quoted him as one of his most influential teachers. His name is Neville Goddard, who wrote as "Neville".

Neville says:

> *The future dream must become a present fact in the mind of him who seeks to realize it. We must experience in imagination what we would experience in reality in the event we achieved our goal [...] affirming that we are already that which we want to be; by assuming the feeling of the wish fulfilled [...] Feeling is the ferment without which no creation is possible.*

These extraordinarily compelling words from Neville tie in with what you have been studying – what the subconscious perceives as true, it reflects in your outer world as a physical manifestation. Now that you know what must be done, the next step is to learn how it is done, and the final step is to do it. The rest of **Part III: Set in Motion Your Infinite Riches,** helps you learn the different methods to instill the perfect pattern; it includes numerous real-life examples as well.

Heart of the Matter

The corollary of the Law of Cause and Effect is a powerful frame of reference to appreciate the rationale of getting on *that* frequency.

19.
GET ON *THAT* FREQUENCY: IMAGINATION (VISUALIZATION)

19. GET ON *THAT* FREQUENCY: IMAGINATION (VISUALIZATION)

Imagination is more important than knowledge. Knowledge is limited whilst imagination encircles the world.

Albert Einstein

When a towering intellectual like Einstein speaks of imagination as superior to knowledge, not only should it reinforce your efforts to further develop this faculty, it should also give you reason to be pleased that you are headed in the right direction.

The origins of the word imagination comes from the Latin *imaginari*, meaning to make a picture to oneself. In other words, think of it as creating images in your mind; think of imagination and visualization as synonymous.

You will now learn more about Neville, who taught the imagination method in a distinct and remarkable manner.

Born in 1905, of English ancestry in Barbados, Neville traveled to the US at the age of eighteen to develop his career as a dancer in the theater. Things did not quite progress as he had hoped, and life was difficult financially for young Neville. However, Neville stumbled upon a book on metaphysics, and in 1931 found himself attending a lecture in New York City by a mysterious Ethiopian seer called Abdullah. At the end of the lecture, Abdullah said, "Neville, you are six months late."

Astounded, Neville said, "I am six months late, but I do not even know you. How do you know me?" Abdullah replied, "The brothers told me." For the next six years, Neville studied with Abdullah the esoteric and deeper meanings of the Bible, Kabbalah, and conscious manifestation to create his reality. It is often said that true learning and mastery occur when you experience something rather than just study it – it was no different for Neville either.

About two years into his training with Abdullah, in October 1933, Neville had an urge to go to Barbados and spend Christmas with his family, but did not have the finances to buy the ticket for the voyage. Neville explained this to Abdullah, who said, "You are in Barbados." Neville replied, "What do you mean, I am in Barbados?" Abdullah responded, "Sleep at night and walk in the day in Barbados." What Abdullah meant – and what Neville did – was imagine and consequently see the world at night from his New York bed as he would if he were sleeping in his Barbados bed. Neville also saw Barbados when walking the streets of New York, as if he were walking the streets of Barbados in the day.

This continued for about a month, into the latter part of November, when Neville started to get impatient and said to Abdullah, "I really want to go to Barbados but despite doing what has been asked of me, there is no sign of the money coming and me going there for Christmas." This annoyed Abdullah who, in turn, retorted, "Haven't I told you that you are in Barbados? You went to Barbados by ship traveling first class and will soon be making your journey back to New York." Having said that, Abdullah slammed the door and left the room with a clear message to Neville not to follow him or discuss the matter further.

About a fortnight later, on December 4, 1933, one evening as Neville returned to his tiny, rented quarters, he found an envelope pushed under the door with a note from his brother that the family wanted him to come over for Christmas and that he should collect his ticket from the shipping company. The envelope also had $50 for Neville to buy clothes, etc., as he prepared for the journey. Neville was ecstatic and the next morning quickly went to collect his ticket, which he got but was told that a part of the journey would not be first class because of availability. Undeterred and still excited, Neville reached Abdullah's home and said that Abdullah was right, he was set to sail the next day, December 6, 1933, but that he was going only partially first class. At this point, Abdullah repeated what he had said earlier: "You are not going because you already are in Barbados… and you went first class. There is nothing else to discuss about this matter and I look forward to seeing you back in New York!" The next day, when Neville reached the ship to sail, he was pleasantly surprised to hear from the staff that there was a last-minute cancellation and that he would be traveling first class.

You should think of this as Neville's debut experience, where he went through a live example of applying the knowledge of what he was studying with Abdullah. This episode changed something within Neville, and he then knew that the solution to his desires was within him and not in the outside world.

Neville wrote more than ten books and gave numerous lectures. There are multiple examples in his works of using imaginative power to manifest the desired result. These examples include both Neville's personal experiences and those of his students.

Now that you have learnt about Neville, it will be useful to take a step back and really understand how imagination enables the manifestation of desires. In our physical world, as you now know, manifestation is a real-time function of the pattern frequency in the subconscious mind. The wonderful part here is that you have this latent power and ability to instill the relevant pattern as much as Neville did. In Neville's case, this developed through disciplined training and study over time and, in your case, it can as well if you undertake such disciplined study and training.

This is where it gets most interesting because we as human beings typically think in images. There have been many studies done in this context over the decades, but a relatively recent one at Harvard found that even when people were prompted to use verbal thinking, they created visual images to accompany their inner speech, suggesting that visual thinking is deeply ingrained, while speech is a relatively recent evolutionary development. Images are also a powerful medium to distill from the conscious into the subconscious mind.

Thanks to their study and training, people such as Abdullah and Neville are able to get on *that* frequency through the power of imagination in a relatively short time and, consequently, manifest swiftly compared to others. Such people have mastered two critical qualities. **First, while imagining, they think from the position of their desire fulfilled dwelling in them.** They do not think of their desire fulfilled as separate from them. This is a compelling concept, originally suggested by Neville.

This difference is evident in the Barbados–New York example. Neville, while going to bed, saw in his imagination the view from his Barbados bed, and in the day, when he walked in New York, he saw the streets of New York as if he were seeing the streets of Barbados. **Neville did not imagine or visualize the experience; he instead lived the experience.**

The second quality is their unequivocal faith around the achievement of their desire. They have absolute faith and NO doubt in the fulfillment of their desire – they trained and studied so as not to let their physical senses cast doubt around the feeling of the fulfillment of their desire just because it was not yet manifested.

Most importantly, remember you too can develop these qualities over time with discipline and the right guidance. I want you to thoroughly understand the difference between imagining while thinking of the desire fulfilled versus thinking from the position of the desire fulfilled.

The best analogy I can share with you is Neville's ladder. In the ladder analogy, Neville says if your desire is to climb the ladder and you see yourself climbing the ladder, then you are thinking **of** the desire fulfilled. On the contrary, when you feel your feet on the top two rungs of the ladder – your hands holding the rails to get there – and you see the view from the top of the ladder, then you are thinking **from the place of** the desire fulfilled.

In practice, what is most effective is to create a scene of about five to fifteen seconds, which captures the feeling of the wish fulfilled. The prerequisite is that this scene can only happen once your desire has manifested. Additionally, the scene must be one you view the world from and not one where you think of the scene and see yourself fulfilling it. Both the New York–Barbados and ladder examples reinforce this approach.

Having understood these rules, and to get you started, now think of the dream car you would love to drive. The ideal Neville imagination method would look something like this: (i) See the car in entirety in the color you want, parked where you want it. Feel your hand open the door and feel yourself sitting down in the driver's seat. (ii) See your wrist, forearms, and the view from the driver's seat as you drive this car on your street. (iii) Feel your hands on the steering wheel. (iv) Feel the smell of the new leather in the car. **(v) Most importantly, feel the thrill of driving this car as a natural, everyday event in your life – it is not a big deal!**

I have written these sub-steps in this car example so that you can soak up the ingredients for a successful imagination session using Neville's teachings.

A personal, real-life example follows next, and then you end the chapter with an exercise.

Finding My Publisher

When I had the first working draft of this book complete, my next task was to find a reputable hybrid publisher globally (except for the Indian subcontinent) whom I felt comfortable working with. I was specifically focused on a hybrid publisher, not a self-publisher or a traditional one.

For about a month, multiple times a day, with dedication, discipline, and strong feeling, through my imagination I generated the feeling that I had found this publisher. I did not take any action at this stage, but just kept doing the imagination exercise. With each passing day, the feeling consistently kept getting stronger and eventually got to a stage where I started to feel that this was done and was not a big deal. It was only then that I started to search online, and within five minutes, Rowanvale Books (https://www.rowanvalebooks.com) stood out as the obvious choice.

What did my imagination exercise entail, you might ask? The exercise was about ten seconds of saying to myself, "Yippee – best hybrid publisher, done!" I did this exercise two or three times a day, and each time did four or five repetitions of about ten seconds each.

I have been doing such imagination exercises for a good number of years, and while all elements of Neville's principles are there, it might appear on the face of things that I have not incorporated all principles. On the contrary, I have, but rather than viewing a scene such as in the ladder example, I have directly gone to generating the feeling. When you start out, as I did at one point, you typically need a particular scene to generate that feeling. However, as you evolve and advance your skills, you can often (still not necessarily always, though) go straight to the feeling generation stage rather than enacting a scene. My suggestion is that you should not rush to get there; let it unfold naturally as you continue to develop on your chosen trajectory.

Let's digress a little and complete the story with what was going on with Cat Charlton (Managing Director, Rowanvale Books) before I contacted her. Just as there is a frequency match between your pattern and its physical manifestation, it is also a frequency match when people find each other for a common cause!

Physically based in London as I was "searching" for this hybrid publisher, 150 miles (250 km) away, near Newport in Wales, was a hybrid publisher searching for a certain "someone". This "someone" was ideally a person who had natural values that matched Cat's, and could use their experience to mentor her to develop Rowanvale to the next level. Part of Cat's desire was driven by wanting to make a bigger impact, and part by the practicality of her younger child shortly starting nursery, so freeing up her time.

I never knew any of this until much later, when we exchanged notes on how we have both played such an important part in each other's lives, how we met at just that right moment, and how there are no coincidences – what/whom you search for also searches for you. What adds to the perfection here is that my first email to Cat was on her younger son's third birthday!

Exercise 1

Bearing in mind what a strong imagination scene looks like, conceptualize such a scene based on your Primary Vision and play it on the screen of your mind between five and ten times. Be relaxed and sit comfortably in a quiet place. People often use a meditative posture, but this is not compulsory. When complete, note how you felt when you did this exercise.

_____

_____

_____

Heart of the Matter

Bob Proctor said, *Imagination is the greatest nation* – I couldn't agree more. Become a citizen of this nation, and you will reap the abundant benefits it has to offer.

20.
GET ON *THAT* FREQUENCY: VISION BOARD

20. GET ON *THAT* FREQUENCY: VISION BOARD

The only person you are destined to become is the person you decide to be.

Emerson

A vision board is a physical or digital collection of images that help generate the feeling of your manifestation as complete. Continuing with the car example from the last chapter, the ideal vision board would be one that has images of your car in the color you desire, parked where you would like it to be, with you in the driver's seat, you standing next to it, and so on and so forth.

To maximize the benefit of vision boards, the best approach is to find and/or create between three and ten images that generate the feeling of already having manifested your desire. You can go with just one or two images if you feel most comfortable that way, but at the other end of the spectrum, anything more than ten starts to spread the impact too thinly.

Once you have the images, then either physically or digitally position them on a single page. The principal requirement is to have them all placed around each other such that they collectively magnify the final impact. I also recommend writing your Primary Vision somewhere in the middle of the vision board.

Every time you look at your vision board, it should serve one objective – to boost within you the feeling of having manifested your desire. Often, when new students start these exercises, they soon get comfortable with their vision board because the images already exist physically.

You will now read two real-life examples of the results of vision boards and then do your own vision board exercise.

My Home

The most personal example of successful use of a vision board is that of my current home. My wife and I were keen to buy our next home on a particular street which, at the time, did not have a property on the market. Not wanting to compete or forcibly lay a claim to what belonged to someone else, I downloaded the headline photo of the last property sold on the street and looked at it every day, giving thanks for a similar property on the street. I also contacted the estate agent who sold the last property, requesting that when a home on that street came on the market, she should let me know before advertising it to the wider audience, and that would save costs all round.

While nothing happened for the first two months, in August 2019, in the middle of the summer holidays, the estate agent made contact saying that the owners of the house next to the one last sold were keen to sell and were in a hurry. It transpired that their daughter, through a somewhat unusual chain of events, had bought her ideal home and, in the process, moved about thirty miles away from her parents. This was difficult for the parents, the daughter, and the grandchild. The parents also said they had been thinking over the years that, as they got older, they wanted to move closer to the country and out of the hustle and bustle of a London suburb, but had never got down to doing it – their daughter's move now was the perfect reason to take this step.

What was even more intriguing was that they had almost overnight found a chain-free home on the street next to their daughter's, and because they needed to sell their current home to buy the other one, they were given a fortnight by the seller to confirm they had a buyer, else the property would be back on the market. Furthermore, when they told the estate agent about their situation, their request was to find a ready and reliable buyer very quickly to whom they were willing to give a nominal discount on the asking price if it avoided putting their property officially on the market!

As expected, it all fell into place smoothly; we purchased the home at a small discount, additional costs of officially putting on the market were avoided, the sellers got their preferred home, and the estate agent received a fine bottle of vintage wine – a true win-win-win situation all round!

Now for the most fascinating part of the story. When the transaction completed, feeling rather nostalgic and grateful, I went back to see the vision board. It was then that it dawned on me that because of the angle of the photo, the maximum focus was on the house next to the one that had sold! Accordingly, every day for those two months I had been looking at the neighboring house a lot more than the one I thought I was looking at, and it eventually became my forever home.

John Assaraf's Home

Talking of homes, another vision board example is that of John Assaraf. John is a respected personal development practitioner, and it was through his work many years ago that I first learnt about vision boards. They instantly clicked for me, and I haven't stopped using them since!

In John's case, he created his vision board and put it up on his office wall. Thereafter, he saw himself already enjoying the object of his desire. A few years later, when he moved homes, his son noticed a stack of boxes and asked him what was inside them. John told his son that the boxes contained his vision boards. He then proceeded to open the boxes for his son and when he saw one particular board, he started crying because on it were photos of his dream house – and it was the very same home he was now living in!

Exercise 1

To start with, identify between three and ten images which generate within you the thrill of having manifested your Primary Vision. If it feels natural, add the text of your Primary Mission and Vision. Then, look at it for two to three minutes, and pen down how you feel when you look at it.

Heart of the Matter

A vision board is the physical equivalent of an imagination exercise on the screen of your mind. Unlike imagining or visualizing, it is already physically there, putting this method at a relative advantage.

21.
GET ON *THAT* FREQUENCY: MIND MOVIES®

21. GET ON *THAT* FREQUENCY: MIND MOVIES®

How would you feel if I told you there is a method whereby you could make a mini movie based on your vision board, and add audio and text to it? Most probably, you would just love the idea – happy days then, because this is exactly what Mind Movies® does!

Using sound and words in addition to images, Mind Movies® combines the best features of both imagination and vision boards, resulting in a mammoth impact to manifestation. Simply defined, a Mind Movie® is a two-to-three-minute customized mini video of your ideal life, dreams, and desires. You have a choice to use either a series of images with background music or a series of video-audio clips; these can further be supplemented with text or affirmations displayed on the screen. The best features of Mind Movies® are that your movie is entirely customized by you, for you, and appeals to your mind through multiple avenues – images, sounds, and words; it truly is a 21st-century technology version of visualization, combining the best of traditional imagination, vision boards, sound, and text.

Mind Movies® had its origin more than a decade ago when a young man in Australia made a video representative of his ideal life. He initially made this video because he was embarrassed when friends would come over and see his old-school vision board with his big dreams and goals. Every time he showed others this video, though, they thought of it as fun, cool, and exciting. Because the reaction to his video was consistently positive and encouraging, he approached his friends Natalie and Glen Ledwell to start an online business with him to empower people around the world to make such movies for themselves.

Natalie and Glen worked tirelessly, expanding this idea over the years to reach more than ten million people as of April 2024. Scaling up this idea in a relatively short time with limited means and experience was not without its challenges. However, Natalie and Glen diligently used (often multiple times a day) a Mind Movie® they had generated, representing the successful launch of Mind Movies®, in order to launch with aplomb Mind Movies® to a global audience!

You will have guessed by now why Mind Movies® is such a phenomenal tool to use. By using images, sound, and text, it appeals to multiple senses. In terms of examples, if I were to list the number of people I know who use Mind Movies®, I would need more than a page! I have used Mind Movies® over the years and found it most beneficial. Furthermore, signing up is affordable and simple, membership is for life, and you can make multiple movies as and when you like.

Exercise 1

Once you've read through the entire book, register on the Mind Movies® website https://www.mindmovies.com (or the upgraded version of the software https://platinum.mindmovies.com/#/) and create an initial movie. The primary objective at this stage is to ascertain how you feel when you see your movie – you can always improvise and make more Mind Movies® in future. Do make a note of the feeling this generates when you watch it.

_____

_____

_____

Heart of the Matter

Mind Movies® is a powerful method incorporating the best features of imagination, vision boards, music, and text – make the most of it.

22.
GET ON *THAT* FREQUENCY: AFFIRMATIONS

22. GET ON *THAT* FREQUENCY: AFFIRMATIONS

It is the repetition of affirmations that leads to belief, and once that belief becomes a deep conviction, things begin to happen.

Claude Bristol

An affirmation, as the name suggests, is a statement you make to yourself as true. It is a powerful route to the subconscious mind using the strength of words. When these words are repeated using specific rules, they are persuasive in the development of new patterns. There are four compulsory and two suggested rules to heighten the impact of affirmations.

The compulsory rules are:

- Your affirmation must be spoken and not just thought to yourself.

- Your affirmation must be in the present tense and affirm that what you desire is already yours. The best way to start is with "I am…"

- Your affirmation must be brief and simply worded.

- Your affirmation must generate the feeling of already having manifested what you desire.

The suggested rules are:

- While saying your affirmation, look at yourself in the mirror. Try to get visual alignment between your eyes and their reflection in the mirror.

- In addition to "I am", start with giving thanks for your affirmation as already true. For example, say "I am so grateful because…"

Let's take an example and assume that your desire is to have a net worth of $2 million.

Your perfect affirmation, looking at yourself in the mirror and generating the feeling of your net worth already being $2 million, should be: **"I am so grateful because my net worth is $2 million."**

Like the other methods you have learnt, affirmations must generate within you the feeling of already having manifested what you desire. That is the paramount reason why affirmations should be in the present tense.

There are two approaches to fruitfully using affirmations. The first is the traditional approach, like with the $2 million net worth example. The second is a bit more innovative and is what I personally use and often recommend. With this latter approach, rather than going for a targeted affirmation, use a somewhat general affirmation, which is in a setting after you have manifested your desire. For example:

(i) *I am so grateful because all my desires manifest swiftly on an ongoing basis.*

(ii) *I am so grateful because my Primary Vision has swiftly manifested.*

There are two examples from different periods in my life, about ten years apart, which I would love to share with you. The first goes back to the end of 2010 and the early part of 2011, while the latter is much more recent, from April 2023.

In the first example, I was employed with a multinational bank in London, in a role focused on the African market. The senior management felt that to be most productive in that role, I should move to Africa for a year. I was not keen to. I discussed this with the management and was told that while the Africa-based role would pay me much more than London, if I wanted to continue with the role, then I would need to move. To make matters worse, there wasn't a similar role based in London at that point.

I was very keen to be based in London and, for the next three months, every day kept affirming to myself upwards of fifty, and sometimes 100, times a day: "I am permanently based in London." I chose to ignore the external factors around my African visa application, conversations with the local team there, and other similar activities. Instead, I chose to walk in the feeling of the wish fulfilled, as though I were permanently living in London. I enrolled my two-year-old in the local nursery, started looking for a new apartment to rent and, above all, just went about my daily life as though I were based here forever.

Fast forward to the Christmas build-up in December 2010. I received a phone call from HR confirming that for the first time since they could check the records, it appeared that a residential work visa had been rejected and that there did not seem to be an appeals process in place! An hour later, I got a second call, this time from the Head of our Department, saying that there had been a most unexpected resignation "coincidentally" around the same time as my visa decision was relayed. Furthermore, the hiring manager for the new role was someone who thought well of me, knew my reluctance to go to Africa, and wanted to offer me the London-based role to replace the person leaving. It was indeed a momentous Christmas…

The second example is relatively recent – April 2023 – about 5,000 miles from London in sunny New Delhi. As we were getting set for the annual April ritual of the kids meeting the grandparents, as happens every Easter break (except the two Covid years), I started to notice a growing desire developing within me to meet someone there who had the same intention to serve others… and explore how that person could play a part, especially in India, with my vision for the **Centre for Infinite Riches**®.

In this instance, I used the simplest possible affirmation, giving thanks saying: "Thank you for this person." I said it about fifty times a day but did not take any action at that stage nor when we started the holiday; I just went about my holiday with the feeling of the wish fulfilled.

About four days after we got there, with the temperature at 37°C or about 100°F, the children started to insist that they wanted to spend half a day at an outdoor pool. The next day, we arrived at the Eros Hotel in Nehru Place, which is a fifteen-minute drive from our family home in New Delhi. My wife did not join us, and as the sole parent-in-charge, once the children were safely in the pool, I got myself a chilled beer and sat down in a corner, just thinking about life and this person.

My thoughts were interrupted by the lifeguard, Sunil Kumar (https://in.linkedin.com/in/sunil-kumar-4656272a), who walked up to me and said hello. I reciprocated the greeting and we started to chat, exchanging pleasantries, and discussing the weather as we got to know each other a bit more. Once the conversation gravitated towards what we both did for a living, he said something to me, and at that moment I knew I had found the person I was searching for!

Sunil said that while he enjoys what he does and does his best for every customer who comes to the pool area, he rarely walks up to a guest and starts chatting as he did with me. He could not quite fathom why he'd done so, but somehow knew that he just had to. He then asked me if we could try to unravel why he'd had this urge to speak to me.

As we spoke further, Sunil said that he is happiest when serving people, and he likes his job at the poolside, yet has this strong desire to serve people at a much larger scale than just at the pool.

We spent the next hour discussing the **Centre for Infinite Riches**®, my vision, and how he represented the person I wanted to meet during this visit. He was delighted and said that he couldn't get over the coincidence. In turn, I told him that there are no coincidences and explained – as simply as I could for a first timer by the poolside with a beer in one hand – the frequency match between us!

I share these two personal examples so that they can help you consolidate your understanding of the wonderful manifestation method of affirmations. Bear in mind, though, that as with the other methods, the affirmation must ignite within you the feeling of already having manifested your desire.

Exercise 1

Using the suggested rules, and lessons from the examples shared, draft two affirmations of your own. Once drafted, say them out loud between ten and twenty times. You don't have to scream but avoid trying to whisper! If possible, find a mirror where you can look at yourself when you say them. Once completed, make a note of what feeling these affirmations generated within you.

Heart of the Matter

Affirmations are a powerful technique using the strength of words, and using them while following the rules in this chapter will enhance their impact.

23.
GET ON *THAT* FREQUENCY: MISCELLANEOUS METHODS

23. GET ON *THAT* FREQUENCY: MISCELLANEOUS METHODS

Whatever the mind can conceive and believe, it can achieve.

Napoleon Hill

I have clubbed these methods together in one chapter under the "miscellaneous" category, not because they are less powerful or significant than the ones you have studied so far, but because they are relatively quicker and more concise to explain, and I felt you would benefit most in this format.

(I) I-to-Me Letter

I just love writing a letter to myself! It is something I discovered about five years ago and have been partial to ever since. There are four key features of such a letter. (i) Date: This should be the date when you think your desire would have manifested. (ii) Content: This should include sentences that reinforce how you feel now that your desire has manifested. (iii) Length: Preferably between five and ten lines. (iv) Tense: Write your letter as if your desire has already manifested.

Cat Charlton very much liked the idea of the innovative affirmation and developed a high degree of comfort putting it to good use. However, she went a step beyond when I introduced her to the I-to-Me Letter; she got a brainwave to combine the best features of the innovative affirmation and the letter.

Her letter reads as follows:

April 11, 2027

The most special birthday so far it has been! I have been consistently living my Primary Missions, and Primary Visions have all swiftly manifested. I am now busy working on the next set of Primary Visions and feel so overwhelmed with gratitude for all that has been achieved.

Exercise 1

Drawing on the key features of the I-to-Me Letter, and guided by Cat's example, draft your own I-to-Me Letter, then read it three or four times and note the feeling it ignites in you.

(II) Primary Vision Card and Physical Objects

A Primary Vision Card is a plain white card the size of a standard business card on which you write your Primary Mission on one side and your Primary Vision as already manifested on the other. You can opt to leave out the Primary Mission and just go with the Vision on both sides. Most importantly, you must leave this in your pocket or keep it somewhere you will either touch or see it multiple times a day.

The fundamental premise is that you are using a touchy-feely written method that reminds you many times a day about already having manifested your Primary Vision, and so hastens the pace of the outward physical manifestation.

Everybody puts their hands in their pocket or wallet several times a day and, if each time you put your hand there you touch that card, you are briefly but continuously reminding yourself of having manifested your Primary

Vision. Moreover, if you have the card with you all day, then whenever you have a spare minute or so, you can give it a quick read as well.

This method is most advantageous because it is the least time-consuming of all methods, does not need you to go to a silent or private place, and helps you remind yourself upwards of ten times a day.

A supplement to the card is the concept of physical objects. This method entails keeping in your office or bedroom (or any room where you spend a good amount of time) physical objects that remind you of your Primary Vision. If you are on the move often, then it might be best to give this method a miss.

One example here is a plaque on which is written your Primary Vision as already manifested. Another option is photos or small figurines of people who motivate you and like whom you aspire to be – these mostly would be leaders in your field who have achieved similar Primary Visions to yours. Finally, like with the card, the stand-out feature of this method is the ease to access it, with repeated reminders every day as you go about your daily activities.

It is a date I think I'll remember for a long time: December 24, 2022 – a typical, festive, Christmas eve. I'd received delivery of my shiny new HP laptop that morning and spent most of the afternoon designing the logo for the **Centre for Infinite Riches®**.

With the first draft of my logo designed, and daylight starting to give way to dusk on the shortest day of the year, my laptop, a glass of one of my preferred red wines (Château Sirène, Saint-Julien, Bordeaux), and I made our way to my office in the garden. I settled down on my chair and intently looked at the framed portraits of my four mentors, asking for inspiration. This went on for about half an hour – just the four of them and me in this on-and-off, locked-gaze mode. As the minutes ticked by, I gradually started to feel clearer about what I wanted to write on my Primary Vision Card and, before the flow was broken, quickly wrote down my thoughts.

What I wrote hasn't changed since, and the card stays in my pocket. The points on the card are:

(i) The Centre is present in all continents (ii) The Centre is a well-respected, global personal development brand (iii) Manifest Your Infinite Riches is a bestseller available in more than 100 countries (iv) My work has "woken up" four million people (v) My net worth is $X

Dated: October 21, 2026

As of the end of 2024, from the list above, the first point has already manifested, while the second and third appear all set to be realized by the middle of 2025. For both the fourth and fifth, the feeling within me is that these are already real… and I am confident these will also manifest before the due date.

Additionally, beyond the card, I do quite enjoy using physical objects in my **Centre for Infinite Riches**® office. The best example (as I alluded to on the previous page) is the framed portraits of my four mentors in the personal development industry on the wall opposite my chair, behind my desk.

Exercise 2

For this exercise, get your hands on whatever is easily available at home – it could be the back of a regular business card, it could be a blank card if you have one, or else just a small shape cut out from a sheet of paper, about the size of a standard business card. Using the information in this chapter, create the first draft of your own Primary Vision Card. Read it multiple times and note what it makes you feel. Moreover, if there is a physical object easily available at home, hold it, look at it, and note how you feel.

(III) Listening

The listening method, as the name suggests, is about listening to something that generates for you the feeling of already having manifested your Primary Vision. There are two different methods within the "listening" category which can intensify your manifestation experience.

The first is regularly listening to a song that puts you in the frame of mind wherein you are reminded of living your Primary Mission and fulfilling your Primary Vision.

The second is recording your voice and repeatedly listening to one or two lines that imply that your desire has already manifested. These could be an affirmation, the text of the card, or a line or two taken from the I-to-Me Letter.

Through my childhood and beyond, I haven't really been a musically-inclined person. However, over the last few years, I just "happened" to listen to some old songs that I have not been able to stop listening to since! Of course, nothing just happens, and my frequency was one which got these songs into my life at the time I was ready. I have since embraced them and can never seem to get enough of them. The English language ones are *'I Can See Clearly Now'* by Johnny Nash and *'Somewhere Over the Rainbow'* by Israel Kamakawiwoʻole. The Bollywood ones are *'Ek Din Bik Jayega, Matee Ke Mol'* and *'Jeena Yahan, Marna Yahan'* by Mukesh, for roles played by Raj Kapoor. With all these songs, the blend of the lyrics and the music stirs something within me which, for want of a better expression, "amplifies on steroids living my Primary Mission and fulfilling my Primary Vision!"

The second example is of my younger daughter, Mayra. Mayra was eight years old when the pandemic was at its peak. The combination of the pandemic, homeschooling, the house under renovation, and the London winter did at times make her come to me and say that she was feeling rather sad. Amongst other things to cheer her up, we watched *The Sound of Music*. At the end of the film, I asked her why she thought singing *'I Have Confidence'* gave Julie Andrews the confidence to do a good job. Mayra's untainted answer was to say, "Because she convinced herself!" I then told her that she too could convince herself that she was happy when she was sad. While she was still amenable to the idea, we quickly recorded ten repetitions in her voice: "I love my life and I am so happy." I worked with her until homeschooling stopped three months later, the following February, for her to say this whenever she felt sad. It pepped her up many times and often kept her spirits up in those rather difficult times. I have shared this example for you to get a different perspective beyond the Primary Mission and Vision context and see that even an eight-year-old can benefit from this method (and other methods too), when used correctly.

The last example also goes beyond the Primary Mission and Vision and uses more than one method. It so happens that every sensible author knows that no matter how great they think their content is, they would, at the minimum, need the services of an editor; the more enthusiastic authors, though, often use the services of more than one. Likewise, Alan Howarth (https://www.alanhowarthwriter.co.uk) was one of my editors for *Manifest Your Infinite Riches*.

Alan was suffering a fair amount of pain while waiting for a replacement knee operation for his left leg, and reports seemed to suggest it was going to be a rather long wait with the NHS (NHS stands for the National Health Service and is the publicly-funded healthcare system in England).

Using the methods from this chapter, Alan started by picking the date by which he would receive his operation schedule – Thursday, May 11, 2023. He wrote on the card, drafted an I-to-Me Letter, chose his motivational music – The Proclaimers, '*500 Miles*' – and tried to walk in the feeling of the wish fulfilled.

Thursday, May 11, 2023 arrives and, lo and behold, at about 11:00 a.m., the phone starts ringing, and it's the hospital calling to suggest they do the operation within May. This was exceptional, logic-defying news, especially against the backdrop of delays the NHS has faced after the end of the pandemic. Alan was ecstatic, and immediately sent me a message saying, **"It Works - ☺ "**.

Exercise 3

Almost all of us have a song (or two) that puts us in a happy frequency. Start listening to yours and see how it makes you feel. Also record a couple of lines in your voice along the lines suggested and note how you feel when listening to them.

Heart of the Matter

The methods in this chapter are as valuable as those to which entire chapters have been devoted. Are you able to identify a favorite from within this chapter?

PART IV

---------------------------------->

MANIFEST YOUR INFINITE RICHES

<----------------------------------

24.
TAKING
STOCK

24. TAKING STOCK

The journey of a thousand miles begins with a single step.

Lao Tzu

Congratulations! Yes, you are now at the final step, where you will learn to manifest your infinite riches. At the start, in the Introduction, you read that:

Human nature is such that once you know something can be done, half the journey is complete; the other half is about successful application and disciplined execution [...]

Understanding these concepts and ideas is the critical first step, but this in itself will not get you the results; consistent application in putting them to practical use and ensuring disciplined execution are the decisive factors.

All you have studied up to now comprises the first part of learning these concepts and ideas that the Introduction refers to. The last step, on the other hand, is all about the successful application and disciplined execution of the knowledge you have gained. Do not think that just because developing a sound understanding of the concepts fills ninety percent of this book, it is any more important than the last step. Both are equally important, and neither can be fully effective without the other.

You will soon produce your very own **Daily Ritual To Manifest Your Infinite Riches**™. Not only does this Daily Ritual enable you to start manifesting your infinite riches, but it also contributes to you maintaining the manifesting frequency.

Heart of the Matter

With all the knowledge gained and the understanding developed, your sole focus now is to successfully apply this knowledge through disciplined execution on an ongoing basis.

25.
THE TWO
PRINCIPAL SOURCES

25. THE TWO PRINCIPAL SOURCES

It's one thing to feel that you are on the right path, but it's another to think that yours is the only path.

Paulo Coelho

While the manifestation process is the same for everyone, the path to mastering the process differs from person to person. I am yet to come across two people with identical rituals. That is why, rather than share a set of exercises for you to follow, I am helping you create your very own bespoke ritual.

The ingredients of your Daily Ritual are drawn from two principal sources: The Six Manifestation Turbochargers™ and the 3-6-9 Triangle of Manifestation™. It is paramount that you really understand these before you produce your Daily Ritual.

The Six Manifestation Turbochargers™

1. **Gratitude:** Starting your day with a brief prayer of gratitude listing your blessings and significant achievements is a great way to commence a new day on the right frequency. The Law of Cause and Effect puts you in a state of receiving when you come from a place of gratitude. It is this law that makes a feeling of genuine gratitude a turbocharger to manifestation. Ask yourself: if you are giving thanks for your blessings and reminding yourself of your best achievements, then through the Law of Cause and Effect, is it not natural that the blessings and achievements will continue to grow? It was in March 2009, while reading Robin Sharma's book *Who Will Cry When You Die?*, I came across Robin recommending that we follow this advice: *When you send your money out, remember always to bless it. Ask it to bless everybody that it touches, and command it to go out and feed the hungry and clothe the naked, and command it to come back to you a million-fold.* Robin, in turn, cited the source as Al Koran's *Bring Out the Magic in Your Mind.* In the overall scheme of things, one book led to another… and the cycle continued.

2. **Meditation:** Meditation silences the mind and takes you closer to universal spirit. Both

these features are important for you to receive guidance on the next steps in your journey. A powerful example here is that of Jack Canfield seeking guidance on the next steps for his book, *Chicken Soup for the Soul*. As he meditated, Jack saw an image of a thermos with chicken soup in it. This reminded him of his grandma's chicken soup, which she said could cure anything. In that flash of guidance from universal spirit, he christened the book *Chicken Soup for the Soul*.

3. **Study:** Keep some time every day to study so that you enhance your knowledge beyond what you have learnt in this book. A good starting point is the Reference List and Biographies that follow at the end of this book. Feel free to read different books, but often the most effective manifesters read the same material time and again – repetition is key, as you have learnt. One bit of advice here is to have a small set of favorite books (up to five is usually a good number), and while keeping an open mind to new material, you should regularly read your favorite pages/books time and again, ideally daily but at least three or four times a week. The legendary Bob Proctor spent a few minutes every day reading his favorite book *Think and Grow Rich* and enthusiastically extolled that habit to one and all.

4. **Start your day early:** As far as possible, wake up a bit earlier and keep time aside each morning for your Daily Ritual. At times, this might not be possible and, in such cases, based on your wider schedule, the next best option is last thing before sleeping or sometime in the day when you are not distracted. There are many advantages of starting your day early, but I find Robin Sharma's *The 5 AM Club* a valuable read here, and Rumi's words enthralling:

    The breeze at dawn has secrets to tell you [...] ask for what you really want, don't go back to sleep.

5. **The Night Schedule:** The thoughts in the last ten to fifteen minutes before you go to bed at night have an inherent advantage to swiftly reach the subconscious mind and consolidate overnight as you sleep. Accordingly, a miniature version of your morning Daily Ritual is strongly recommended just before you go to bed.

6. **Action:** You have learnt all about the importance of Ongoing Guided Action; considering its significant contribution, it features as one of the Six Manifestation Turbochargers™. As you incorporate into your daily life the methods you have learnt, you will often receive guidance

to act in the form of hunches. Once the initial hunch has come through, while in some instances your intellect will support it, in others, your intellect through the conscious mind will try to rationalize for you why you should not take this action, why it is not logical, and so on and so forth. It does not matter… you must still do it! Remember, nothing moves toward you unless you move toward it.

The 3-6-9 Triangle of Manifestation™

3-6-9 is an exceptional numerological combination, especially in the manifestation sphere. There is some disagreement whether Nikola Tesla first said that 3-6-9 holds the key to the universe; nevertheless, it is a powerful combination to feature prominently in your Daily Ritual.

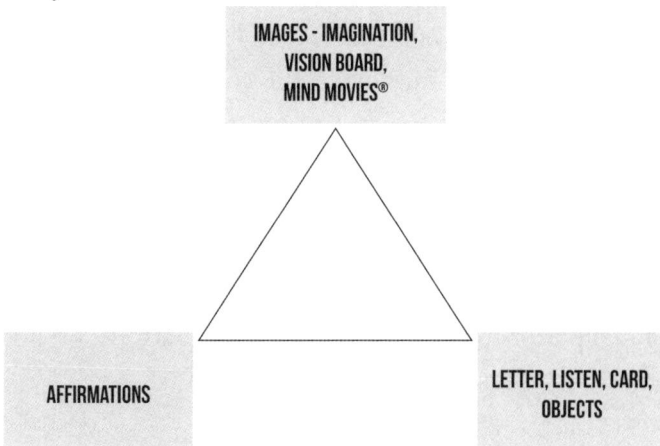

IMAGES - IMAGINATION,
VISION BOARD,
MIND MOVIES®

AFFIRMATIONS

LETTER, LISTEN, CARD,
OBJECTS

I named this the 3-6-9 Triangle of Manifestation™ because the manifestation exercises you will start to do daily will include using these three techniques for nine, six, and three minutes, respectively. These are the techniques you have meticulously studied – now is the time to put them to practical use.

Each exercise you did earlier corresponds to a specific technique in the 3-6-9 Triangle of Manifestation™. As you will remember, after each exercise you made a brief note on how that exercise made you feel.

It is also possible that you feel at this stage that the content you produced during these exercises needs to be improved and/or the Primary Mission and Vision need to be tweaked. My strong suggestion is that you should not fall into the trap of seeking perfection at the cost of a delayed start. This is a problem that every diligent student is prone to, and that is why I am highlighting it now. You can keep improving the content at any time, but do not do so at the cost of not starting your Daily Ritual. Finalize the ritual and start to execute it with discipline every day, from this evening or tomorrow morning. That is the best advice I can give you – if it means you can make a start, partially perfect execution is far superior to perfect planning. Alternatively, do not fall into the paralysis by analysis trap!

Now, assign a score out of ten to every method you practiced through the exercises. The more effective you find a technique, the higher the score. To give you some added perspective, I share below my own scores. Read through those and then complete your table that follows right after.

Pushkar's Table

Technique	Score out of 10
Imagination/Visualization	8
Vision Boards	10
Mind Movies*	10
Affirmations	9
I-to-Me Letter	10
Listening – Your Voice	5
Listening – Your Song	10
Primary Vision Card	8
Physical Objects	10

Put your name here:

_____ **Table**

Technique/Method	Score out of 10
Imagination/Visualization	
Vision Boards	
Mind Movies®	
Affirmations	
I-to-Me Letter	
Listening – Your Voice	
Listening – Your Song	
Primary Vision Card	
Physical Objects	

The subconscious mind is most amenable to images, and in the 3-6-9 Triangle of Manifestation™, I would recommend keeping the nine minutes for images. Whether you find your Mind Movie® useful or if you are yet to devise your Mind Movie®, either way, I would urge you to keep at least four to six minutes for your Mind Movie® because it appeals to multiple senses. Split the rest between your Vision Board and Neville-style imagination, or go with just one method, depending on your scores. I do four minutes for my Mind Movie®, three minutes for my Vision Board and two minutes for the Neville-style imagination.

176 | MANIFEST YOUR INFINITE RICHES

With your images done, it is essential you know which technique you find superior between Affirmations on the one hand and the I-to-Me Letter and/or Listening on the other. The one you prefer is the one that will account for the six-minute slot, and the other for the final three-minute slot. While I am amenable to Affirmations, Listening does not excite me much, but the I-to-Me Letter is a mega-manifester. Accordingly, I devote six minutes to the I-to-Me Letter and three minutes to Affirmations.

Lastly, while the Primary Vision Card and Physical Objects are not part of the eighteen-minute ritual, they are significant contributors because of their repetitive nature every day. Accordingly, decide whether one or both in tandem works best for you. For me, the card never leaves my pocket in my waking hours, and the objects permanently stay in my office.

Pushkar's 3-6-9 Triangle of Manifestation™*:

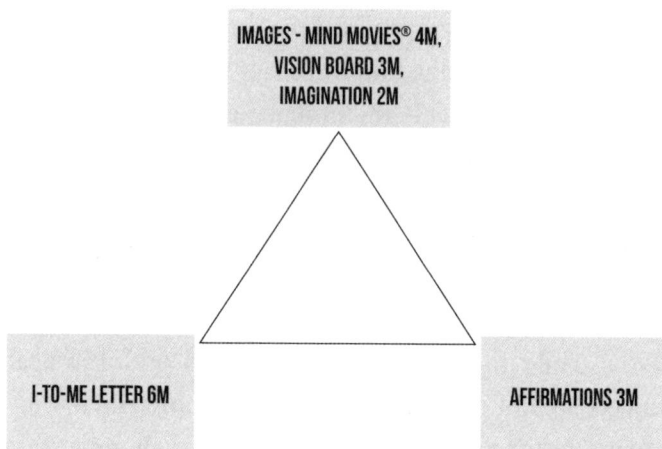

IMAGES - MIND MOVIES® 4M,
VISION BOARD 3M,
IMAGINATION 2M

I-TO-ME LETTER 6M

AFFIRMATIONS 3M

Supported by the Primary Vision Card and Physical Objects outside these eighteen minutes.

Now, complete your 3-6-9 Triangle of Manifestation™.

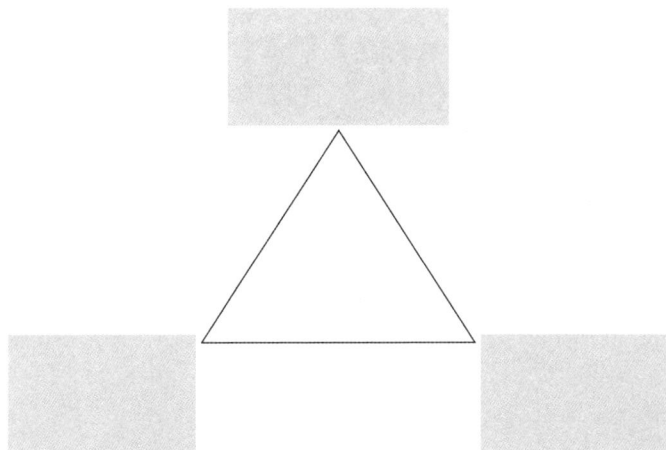

Put your name here:

<u>   </u> **3-6-9 Triangle of Manifestation™*:**

*Supported by the Primary Vision Card and Physical Objects outside these eighteen minutes.

Heart of the Matter

The Six Manifestation Turbochargers™ and the 3-6-9 Triangle of Manifestation™ are key for you to successfully finalize your Daily Ritual.

26.
YOUR DAILY RITUAL TO MANIFEST YOUR INFINITE RICHES™

26. YOUR DAILY RITUAL TO MANIFEST YOUR INFINITE RICHES™

Success is created through the performance of a few small daily disciplines. Failure is the inevitable outcome of a few small acts of daily neglect performed consistently over time.

Robin Sharma

This final chapter starts with this quotation because I want to reinforce the importance of relentless discipline around applying what you have learnt and executing it every day – this is a huge contributor to you manifesting your infinite riches.

Before you complete your **Daily Ritual to Manifest Your Infinite Riches™**, to give you added perspective, I am sharing mine below.

Pushkar's Daily Ritual

Early Morning Ritual

Number	Activity	Duration (minutes)
1.	Expressing Gratitude	5
2.	Meditation	20
3.	3-6-9 Triangle of Manifestation™	9+6+3 = 18
4.	Study	10 to 12
	TOTAL	**53 to 55**

Daytime Activities

Number	Activity	Duration (minutes)
1.	Ongoing Guided Action	Ongoing
2.	Primary Vision Card and/or Physical Objects	Ongoing
	TOTAL	**Ongoing**

Night Ritual

Number	Activity	Duration (minutes)
1.	Expressing Gratitude	2
2.	Meditation	3
3.	3-6-9 Triangle of Manifestation™	3+2+1 = 6
	TOTAL	**11**

Like with anything customized in such a way, while the wider model is the same, the details differ from person to person. I like to meditate for a certain amount of time at a particular time of the day. This does not make it the best option for you. As you start, you might want to keep meditation to ten minutes and studying to five minutes, for example. The core guideline here is that there is no right or wrong combination, and you must do what feels natural and satisfying to you.

Put your name here:

Daily Ritual

Early Morning Ritual

Number	Activity	Duration (minutes)
1.	Expressing Gratitude	
2.	Meditation	
3.	3-6-9 Triangle of Manifestation™	9+6+3 = 18
4.	Study	
	TOTAL	

Daytime Activities

Number	Activity	Duration (minutes)
1.	Ongoing Guided Action	Ongoing
2.	Primary Vision Card and/or Physical Object(s)	Ongoing
	TOTAL	**Ongoing**

Night Ritual

Number	Activity	Duration (minutes)
1.	Expressing Gratitude	
2.	Meditation	
3.	3-6-9 Triangle of Manifestation™	
	TOTAL	

Heart of the Matter

Your journey through this book culminates in the creation of your Daily Ritual – don't just do it, also enjoy it.

27.
CONCLUSION

27. CONCLUSION

If I want to be free, I've got to be me. Not the me you think I should be, not the me I think my wife thinks I should be, not the me I think my kids think I should be. If I want to be free, I've got to be me – so I better know who me is.

Leland Val Van De Wall (and often used by Bob Proctor)

These words reinforce what the Introduction started with: ***Yes, you are infinitely rich; you are infinitely rich, because you are you!***

Your journey to manifest your infinite riches starts with identifying your infinite riches. However, you cannot identify your infinite riches until you know you. The DR^3 Bubble by definition takes you away from you, but this book brings you back to you!

Once you've identified your Primary Mission and taken the first step in the direction of living your *Dharma*, you are then closely back in touch with you... but that is just the beginning. It is your responsibility not to let your proximity with you ever go away – invest in that relationship and you will see the results. The Daily Ritual is the primary means to develop this relationship further and is supported by the exercises you've done, which you can revisit as and when you like.

Just as there are bumps in every journey but you eventually get to your planned destination, so, too, are there bumps in the journey of life. But, if you stay true to the knowledge you have gained from this material, its application, and disciplined execution, you too will get to your destination – you will manifest your infinite riches.

Most often we encounter these bumps when we have an imperfect pattern or have deviated from harmony with universal spirit, or have not taken the Ongoing Guided Action we should have taken. Do not let the bumps discourage you; persevere, and like the skilled pilot navigating through turbulence, come back to the material here or in any other book(s), make the necessary correction(s), and continue in the direction of manifesting your infinite riches.

These bumps can also be necessary steps for you to get to your destination, although it will almost never appear so at the point when they get in your way... it becomes evident in hindsight.

The best words to support this come from Steve Jobs:

You can't connect the dots looking forward; you can only connect them looking backwards. So, you have to trust the dots will somehow connect in your future. You have to trust in something – your gut, destiny, life, karma, or whatever. This approach has never let me down, and it has made all the difference in my life.

On that note, as we get to the end, I am delighted to say that I've shared with you a lot of what I have learnt over the last fifteen years. My sincere intention is for you to benefit immensely from this knowledge and, most importantly, to manifest your infinite riches.

Heart of the Matter

Manifest Your Infinite Riches!

APPENDIX I

BLAINE BARTLETT
(GRANDMASTER B²)

What you did in the future is determining what you will do in the past.

Like me, I reckon you too think this statement sounds somewhat strange, most so when you read or hear it the first time.

I still vividly remember the moment I first heard these words…

I turned forty in 2016, and I recall my wife saying while gifting me a seat at a seminar led by Bob Proctor, "This is a landmark birthday… make it a memorable one." Truly memorable it turned out to be!

It was a two-and-a-half-day seminar and, on the second day, there was a session with a guest speaker whose work I was not acquainted with at that point. His session followed one of those classic, high-octane Bob Proctor sessions, where both Bob and the audience were on fire; not the easiest speaker to follow.

Twinkly blue eyes, dark gray suit, red tie but, above all, a vibration of kindness and compassion which just couldn't be missed – those were the thoughts that flashed through my mind as Grandmaster B^2 – or Blaine Bartlett – came on stage… and then said, "What you did in the future is determining what you will do in the past."

There is a Chinese proverb that says, *When the student is ready, the teacher appears*. Perhaps I was ready, because at the exact moment he said those words, I knew I had found my teacher.

Grandmaster B²'s session was both content-wise and stylistically well-received; to me, the outstanding feature – even more evident after the preceding session – was the prevalent sense of calm and tranquility as he delivered his presentation. It wasn't until later in 2017, when I started to immerse myself in Wayne Dyer's work, that I realized there was something about Wayne that reminded me of Blaine. At that stage, I couldn't put my finger on what that *something* was – except chuckle to myself that even the names rhymed.

As his session concluded, I quickly read about him online and contacted his office, only to sadly learn that Grandmaster B² did not do one-to-one programs anymore. Disappointed, but not deterred, I then explained how I had this "knowing" that he was to be my teacher and, at the minimum, I had to share this fact with him. After going back and forth for a few minutes, it was agreed I would write a brief note explaining why I had this urge to speak to him, and that the note would be shared with him; thereafter, the ball was in his court. We had our introductory call within forty-eight hours.

The conversation flowed along these lines (these conversations are re-constructed based on memory and are representative of the actual dialogue in spirit, rather than being word-for-word transcripts):

Grandmaster B²: Hello Pushkar, how are you?

Pushkar: How am I? I am super-excited because of the conversation to follow, although I can't expect you to be equally excited! Hope you are well and thank you so much.

Grandmaster B²: It is a pleasure. While I might not be as excited as you are, I am really intrigued – in my more than thirty-five-year career in this field, I have never quite had someone send me a message as you did. Tell me, how can I help?

Pushkar: With a Master's degree from both Cambridge and LSE, and a relatively global career, my life has been a "classic textbook success", yet there has been an emptiness urging me on to search. For example, what is the purpose of life in the overall scheme of things? In particular, I feel I am on a quest to seek answers as to why life unfurls as it does for people – especially from the perspective of people finding themselves in one of these situations: (i) Leading fulfilling and financially satisfying lives; (ii) Leading fulfilling but not financially satisfying lives; (iii) Leading empty but financially satisfying lives; (iv) Leading empty and financially lacking lives.

I have been on this quest for the last eight or nine years and, as of last count, enrolled in about twenty seminars, workshops and programs, and read more than 250 books. I certainly have greater clarity than I did when I started; nevertheless, there is this nagging feeling at the back of my mind, which tells me there is something I am meant to do but I cannot seem to decipher what that something is. It is as though a force bigger than me is pulling me in a direction I am happy to get pulled in, and while I do not know the destination, I still somehow know what the next step is – does this make any sense? Furthermore, at an intellectual level, I appear to know that I need a teacher to work with closely but, at a feeling level, I somehow know that teacher is you and that there is not only a larger purpose to fulfill for me but possibly for you as well.

Grandmaster B²: Most interesting, Pushkar – you are analytical, yet you speak authentically from the heart; my intrigue grows. Anyway, as I have gone through life, I have learnt to trust my instinct much more than my intellect, especially in the absence of perfect information. Having spoken to you the last few minutes, listened to you, but *most importantly* felt the energy, I feel comfortable to make an exception and work with you one-to-one.

Pushkar: Thank you so much; I am deeply grateful and promise that you will not be disappointed.

Grandmaster B²: Ha, ha, ha – I think we will both enjoy our conversations very much.

Pushkar: Can't wait to start! Also, if you do not mind my asking… about the fees? From what I have gathered, you do not usually do one-to-one lessons but, in the unlikely event you do, the amount is about $5,000 per hour? This is not something I would be able to afford, but I know I am meant to work with you. What do you suggest is the way around this?

Grandmaster B²: While money is important, we do not do everything for money. I will work with you to help you identify your missing link and help you fulfill your purpose while I unravel how mine is tied to yours. On the financials, feel free to make a charitable contribution aligned to our sessions. If you like, I can recommend a charity I am involved with. My wife, Cynthia, leads a charity called the Unstoppable Foundation, and it has been doing some very good work in parts of rural Kenya.

Pushkar: That sounds fabulous and thank you so much once again – like your intrigue, my gratitude grows. How do we time these sessions? I am bursting with excitement.

Grandmaster B²: I think spreading this over time will be most valuable. My suggestion is monthly sessions of an hour each. These should last for at least twelve to eighteen months, but I have a feeling they will go on for much longer…

Pushkar: I will be guided entirely by your judgment here and will make sure that I come well prepared for the lessons.

Grandmaster B²: There are no lessons! There is no such program or course I run; it will be like an open house for you. Bring your questions, ask me what you like. We can even discuss a particular book or a part thereof, or even a specific quotation. It will be entirely your decision, and I will do my best to oblige. Also, if you don't mind, can I ask how old are you?

Pushkar: All noted and understood; sounds very good. I just turned forty on October 21.

Grandmaster B²: Did you say October 21? And the year, 1976?

Pushkar: Yes – sorry, is something the matter?

Grandmaster B²: No, no… nothing is the matter, but there are no coincidences in this perfect universe, and my intrigue stays on an upward trajectory. You've followed Bob Proctor's work – do you recall him sharing the story of how his life changed when his first mentor, Ray Stanford, handed him a copy of *Think and Grow Rich*?

Pushkar: Yes, I have heard that but, sorry, I still don't understand how that links in with our conversation?

Grandmaster B²: Do you recall when that happened?

Pushkar: 1961, if I remember correctly?

Grandmaster B²: Yes, you are right, but the complete date was October 21, 1961 – wait till I tell Bob about it.

Pushkar: Thank you, but I don't quite know what to say and how to interpret this. Please also can we just keep this between us at this stage?

Grandmaster B²: Yes, of course. Don't worry, this will stay between us until you tell me otherwise. On what this means and how to interpret it, neither of us knows today, but we both will at some point in the future. Most importantly, do remember that neither you finding your way to me nor this conversation that has followed, and the questions you seek, are a coincidence. I don't want to guess the meaning of what has transpired today, and I will ask you not to either. Let's both wait for life to unravel, see what it has in store for you, me, and us, as we now begin the next phase of our quest together...

Pushkar: Thank you, I feel a bit... not sure how to put in words, but not what I expected.

Grandmaster B²: Don't worry, notice what you notice… and let it flow; focus on the experience, not the form.

Pushkar: I love those words – they are now locked into my memory and will stay there forever, as I'm sure lots more will as we start our conversations.

Grandmaster B²: I am pleased to hear that.

Pushkar: Would you mind if I addressed you as Grandmaster B²?

Grandmaster B²: That does sound special… And ah, grand! Yes, I would very much like that.

Pushkar: Thank you.

Grandmaster B²: Thank you for reaching out and for this wonderful conversation I really enjoyed. Oh, one last thing, before we part… You are the first person outside my family I am suggesting this to, but I am because I feel I should.

Pushkar: Thank you, my turn to be intrigued now.

Grandmaster B²: Someone in my extended family has just completed a brief course on numerology and, about the time you made contact, shared this link where we can enter our date of birth and full name and in turn get a simple numerology reading around key personality traits, purpose in life, etc. I didn't know much about this, but we have enjoyed learning a bit more about ourselves the last few days. It seems like a fun exercise and takes a minute to run. Would you like me to do it for you?

Pushkar: Yes, please.

Grandmaster B²: There we go. (*Waits a minute while entering the name and date of birth.*) I will email you the synopsis that is getting generated. Aha, there it is. Very interesting, very interesting... perhaps you were meant to hear this from me today.

Pushkar: Meant to hear this... a bit like the future has already happened, like what you said on stage the other day?

Grandmaster B²: You remember?

Pushkar: Of course, I remember – that is the moment the penny dropped that you are my teacher. Like Abdullah knew Neville was the student, at a different level of awareness, I knew you are my teacher.

Grandmaster B²: I love your authenticity – it is a valuable quality we will delve more into later. On the numbers, apparently your Life Path number is "Nine, The Humanitarian" and your Expression/Destiny number is "Eleven, Master Number".

Pushkar: Thank you, that sounds rather important! I have to admit, I don't know about numerology either, but will invest some time to understand it better. Perhaps it contributes to my quest, which is a part of my life journey?

Grandmaster B²: Perhaps it does. If there is anything you would like to ask me now, then please go ahead.

Pushkar: Nothing at all. Thank you, Grandmaster B².

Grandmaster B²: Now it's my turn to feel important, with that name! It has been an absolute pleasure, Pushkar, and I very much look forward to our next conversation.

Pushkar: Always grateful, and the feeling is mutual, Grandmaster B².

Fast-forward to late 2020 when the world was enveloped in the pandemic, about four years after the preceding conversation. The transcript that follows is from the last of our fifty-or-so sessions spread over four years:

Grandmaster B²: Hello, how are things in London, Pushkar?

Pushkar: Locked up at home, Blaine, and seeing people die every day – not exactly uplifting.

Grandmaster B²: You really are not happy, Pushkar… you called me Blaine, not Grandmaster B².

Pushkar: Apologies, Grandmaster B².

Grandmaster B²: I was just pulling your leg to cheer you up – to cheer up the best student I have had in my forty-year practice. Yes, you have learnt from me, but I have also learnt from you… I know our friendship and relationship is one for life, and this last session is, in some way, just the beginning…

Pushkar: I love you, my dear Grandmaster B², and you know I can never put in words the gratitude I feel for you. I hope Cynthia and you come to London soon, when our home is all sparkling and done, we are ready to sing and dance, Covid is behind us, and we have a memorable two or three days together with you as our guests. Now that your star student is all pepped up, I would say, "You have already visited me!"

Grandmaster B²: Now, that is more like it! On a serious note, as we've discussed a couple of times, your talents, skill set, values, and mindset would make you an effective teacher in the field of personal development. Even the numerology we dabbled in off-and-on in the early days buttresses this premise – this is your purpose, isn't it? Then, why wait? Isn't this the best time, while locked up at home?

Pushkar: Yes, I've thought about it as well and it does really excite me. But I have a request, which is that you also take my advice around the "Wayne-Blaine Bridge" we've discussed. Just as you see me as a next-generation personal development teacher, I see you as filling the gap Wayne Dyer's passing five years ago left us with.

Please listen very carefully to what I am about to say next.

Like me, you would know that the content of Wayne's writings transitioned from motivation to spirituality in the 1990s and, thereafter, he never turned back from spirituality. Your work over the decades has centered on the theme of spirituality within the domain of leadership, rather than spirituality for one and all. You have lately, though, felt a pull towards the wider theme of spirituality for one and all, but you are yet to make that leap. I think as you enter your seventies and with all the experience you have, this is the best time to make that leap. And, yes, that similarity I couldn't put in words before – that is the vibration of compassion you both exhibit. The content of what you both say might be different, but the compassion exuded is rather similar.

On the other hand, I am conscious that most of the work you've done over the course of your life has been outside the US, most so in a Japanese context, and that, unlike Wayne, whose work served the general public and made him a household name, your practice has served a different set of people, meaning you have been relatively hidden from the general public. But, my dear Grandmaster B², with all the wisdom you've gained over the years, and me reminding you multiple times of the

"Wayne-Blaine Bridge", now is the time for you too to start your transition. The bridge is ready – you just need to start walking on it.

Today, four years after our first conversation, I can tell you that our respective purposes are tied in with each other's – you in the form of my teacher, putting me in the direction of mine, and me in the form of your student, nudging you towards yours. You see, Grandmaster B², focusing on the experience and not the form is critical… but only until you are in the advanced stage of your journey, when you know the form. Once you know the form, focusing on both the experience and form become important – and your *Dharma* at this stage beckons you, as mine beckons me.

Grandmaster B²: How pleased and proud I feel, hearing you speak. Do you appreciate now when I say the world needs to hear you? If you can show your Grandmaster B² the way – and with the conviction that you do – then can you imagine the difference you could make to the wider audience – the general public?

Pushkar: Thank you, Grandmaster B² – where do you think I should start?

Grandmaster B²: You are a repository of knowledge from your journey of the last twelve years – convert that into a book. The world would love to hear your journey and gain from the knowledge you will share. How does that sound?

Pushkar: It sounds excellent… I love it! What goes in that book, I don't know today, but this much I do know – it will share not just my journey and knowledge, but it will also tell the world about you.

Grandmaster B²: Thank you, my friend, thank you.

Pushkar: Thank you for everything, and I am sure we will speak before Christmas. Take care and speak soon, Grandmaster B².

Grandmaster B²: You take care too, Pushkar, speak soon.

Fast-forward further to September 9, 2023 – Grandmaster B²'s 74th birthday:

Pushkar: Happy birthday, Grandmaster B² – this is the start of your 75th year!

Grandmaster B²: Thank you, Senior Master Pushkar – perhaps a few more grays and by your 50th I will address you, as Grandmaster.

Pushkar: That tickled me… I feel rather important now, on your birthday. This is my birthday gift to you, Grandmaster B² – Appendix I, which I emailed yesterday. Hope you liked it.

Manifest Your Infinite Riches is undergoing the first round of editing as we speak. **Centre for Infinite**

Riches® is already a UK registered trademark and is in the process of becoming one in the US and India. As we agreed, you are Chief Mentor for the **Centre for Infinite Riches**®. Next year, we'll start to share it with the world. In addition to books, I want the **Centre for Infinite Riches**® to do workshops and events, which you and I must host together.

Grandmaster B²: Thank you, my dear friend, thank you… this is the best birthday gift. I absolutely loved it and will wait for it all to unfurl.

Pushkar: I hope you have a wonderful day; we can catch up on the rest later – I don't want to take up your time on your birthday.

Grandmaster B²: Thank you, but you are not taking up time. How are the three girls of your life? Please give them our best, and a big hug from us both.

Pushkar: I absolutely will, and please give Cynthia my best, as well – I know we will meet soon.

Grandmaster B²: Thank you.

Pushkar: Lots to catch up on. How about I make contact after the weekend, and we catch up later next week?

Grandmaster B²: Sounds good.

Pushkar: Excellent – Happy birthday once again, and bye for now.

Grandmaster B²: Thank you and speak next week.

APPENDIX II

BIOGRAPHIES

Every literary source used in this book is referenced in the Reference List that follows Appendix II. Familiarity with the brief biographies shared (and those of any other figures from the wider Reference List you may like to independently obtain) will help you determine whose work resonates most with you, and you would like to study further. This in turn will give you a wider perspective as you set out to manifest your infinite riches.

While it is not feasible to provide the biography of the author of every referenced source, the ones included are those whose work I have studied closely over a period of time and/or there is an element to their work which has significantly impacted my journey.

James Allen (1864–1912)

Writer, thinker, mystic, and his family's sole breadwinner at fifteen, James Allen's masterpiece, *As a Man Thinketh*, continues to be a popular personal development classic more than a century after his death. Alongside his administrative day job, Allen authored several books and published a spiritual periodical as well. Allen was also amongst the pioneers to promote Eastern spirituality, including Buddhism.

Blaine Bartlett (Grandmaster B²)

Executive coach, leadership development expert, and management consultant, Grandmaster B^2 was instrumental in the founding of the coaching industry in Japan and China, and has authored/co-authored four books, including two bestsellers. Over the course of more than four decades, Grandmaster B^2 has consulted worldwide with executives, companies, and governments, and delivered keynotes and training programs to approximately 300,000 individuals. His website is https://www.blainebartlett.com

Jack Canfield

Founder of the billion-dollar Chicken Soup for the Soul® publishing enterprise, Jack truly is a pioneer and legend in the field of personal development and is globally perhaps the most recognized face of the industry. Jack is also the author of multiple bestsellers and has the rare distinction of his books having sold more than 500 million copies worldwide. In addition to featuring in *The Secret,* Jack has featured in 1,000+ radio and TV shows. To learn more about Jack and his work, please visit https://www.jackcanfield.com

Mike Dooley

Metaphysics teacher, best-selling author, and inventor of *Notes from the Universe*, Mike Dooley is a qualified accountant who had a global career in the corporate sector before transitioning to become an entrepreneur in 1989, when he founded the retail brand TUT (Totally Unique Thoughts). There was a further transition into the field of personal development at the turn of the millennium with the same brand. Since then, Mike has emailed more than one billion *Notes from the Universe* to more than one million people. Mike was also featured in *The Secret*. His website is https://www.tut.com

Wayne Dyer (1940–2015)

Father of motivation, globally renowned author and speaker, Wayne Dyer authored more than forty books, with about half being bestsellers. Wayne transitioned from academia to personal development in the 1970s with his first book, *Your Erroneous Zones,* published in 1976. Over the next fifteen-or-so years, he continued to excel in helping people in their self-improvement journeys. Thereafter, his work progressed more and more to the spirituality genre until his passing in 2015. You can read all about him on https://www. drwaynedyer.com

Neville Goddard (1905–1972)*

Napoleon Hill (1883–1970)

Author of the timeless personal development classic, *Think and Grow Rich*, and Presidential Advisor to Franklin D. Roosevelt, Hill is often thought of as a pioneering contributor to the personal development industry. In 1908, Andrew Carnegie, one of the world's richest men, was being interviewed by the young reporter Napoleon Hill and was so impressed with him that he made him an impromptu offer. The offer was to devote his life to deriving a philosophy of success based on the thinking of the world's richest men, and share that treatise for the benefit of anyone and everyone. Hill took up the offer and took about two decades to complete the "project". The findings were published in 1937 in the book titled *Think and Grow Rich*, which has sold more than 100 million copies and is one of the most successful personal development books of all time. The website of the Napoleon Hill Foundation is https://www.naphill.org

Natalie Ledwell*

---

* For Neville and Natalie, on pages 125-129 and 142, respectively, I have already shared with you the equivalent of what is included for the others in this Appendix. To avoid repetition, while keeping Neville and Natalie at the front of your mind alongside everyone else, their names feature here but the biographies are not repeated.

Mary Morrissey

Inspirational speaker, entrepreneur, and executive coach, for more than four decades Mary has empowered people to progress further on the path of clarifying their dreams and bringing them to life. Mary has spoken three times at the United Nations, facilitated three week-long meetings with His Holiness the Dalai Lama and other world leaders, and met with Nelson Mandela in Cape Town, South Africa, to address the most significant issues our world is facing. She is also the author of two best-selling books. Mary's website is https://www.marymorrissey.com

Bob Proctor (1934–2022)

Personal development guru, mind-master, exceptional speaker, best-selling author, and featured in *The Secret*, Bob Proctor was a towering figure in the field of personal development. From October 21, 1961, when he was given a copy of *Think and Grow Rich*, to the end of his life in the early part of 2022, Bob read a part of *Think and Grow Rich* every day. His legacy continues through his partner, Sandy Gallagher. You can read all about Bob and Sandy at https://www.proctorgallagherinstitute.com

Robin Sharma

Humanitarian, prime leadership expert and speaker, and best-selling author, Robin Sharma transitioned from a legal career to personal development almost thirty years ago. Robin has consulted with multiple Fortune 500 companies, as well as many corporate leaders and CEOs. Over the years, Robin's books have sold more than twenty million copies. His most popular book is *The Monk Who Sold His Ferrari*. You can visit Robin's website at https://www.robinsharma.com

Thomas Troward (1847–1916)

Intellectual, philosopher, and prodigious writer, living more than a century ago, Thomas Troward indeed left his indelible mark in the sphere of New Thought. Amongst the very earliest of New Thought teachers, Troward was perhaps the most known outside the US and was President of the New Thought Alliance. His work is a combination of lectures, essays, and books.

Wallace Wattles (1860–1911)

Philosopher, essayist, and author, Wattles carved a niche for himself amongst the early New Thought authors. While he wrote multiple books and many articles, his seminal work – which continues to inspire people even today – is *The Science of Getting Rich*. From relatively humble beginnings, Wattles read and studied extensively to gain mastery over living a prosperous life. He achieved that prosperity in his later life but died relatively young, aged around fifty.

REFERENCE
LIST

Part I

Chapter 1

- https://guides.loc.gov/this-month-in-business-history/april/apple-computer-founded

- https://www.inc.com/jim-schleckser/apple-s-boring-mission-statement-and-what-we-can-learn-from-it.html

Chapter 3

- Proctor, B., *You Were Born Rich,* LifeSuccess Productions, 1997.

- Wattles, W., *The Science of Getting Rich,* CSA Publishing, 2020.

- Dyer, W., *I Can See Clearly Now,* Hay House, 2014, pp. 133-135.

- Dyer, W., *Your Erroneous Zones,* Piatkus Books, 2009.

Chapter 4

- https://www.visualcapitalist.com/distribution-of-global-wealth-chart

- Kiyosaki, R., *Rich Dad Poor Dad,* Plata Publishing, 2011.

Part II

Chapter 6

- Schwartz, R., *Your Soul's Plan,* Frog Ltd, 2009.

- Dyer, W., *I Can See Clearly Now,* Hay House, 2014, p. 280.

- Chopra, D., *The Seven Spiritual Laws of Success,* Bantam Press, 2022, p. 93.

Chapter 8

- Troward, T., 'Entering into the Spirit of It', *Five Book Collection,* Timeless Wisdom Collection, 2016, pp. 80-83.

- https://www.inc.com/jim-schleckser/apple-s-boring-mission-statement-and-what-we-can-learn-from-it.html

- https://www.canr.msu.edu/news/vision_and_innovation_lessons_from_henry_ford

- https://www.tata.com/newsroom/heritage/jrd-tata-letter-schoolteacher

- https://www.business-standard.com/companies/news/tata-group-retains-top-spot-as-india-s-most-valuable-brand-at-28-6-billion-124062700498_1.html

- https://www.scjohnson.com/en/about-us/this-we-believe

Chapter 9

- Dyer, W., *Wishes Fulfilled,* Hay House, 2012.
- Troward, T., 'The Spirit of Opulence', *Five Book Collection,* Timeless Wisdom Collection, 2016, pp. 65-67.
- Frankl, V., *Man's Search for Meaning,* Rider, 2004.

Chapter 10

- Dooley, M., *Playing the Matrix,* Hay House, 2017.
- Bartlett, B. and Meltzer, D., *Compassionate Capitalism: A Journey to the Soul of Business,* Tisn Media, 2016.
- Proctor, B., *You Were Born Rich,* LifeSuccess Productions, 1997, pp. 3-4.

Chapter 12

- Morita, A., *Made in Japan,* Penguin, 1988, p. 84.
- Dyer, W., *I Can See Clearly Now,* Hay House, 2014, p. 75.

Chapter 13

- https://proctorgallagherinstitute.com/money/how-anyone-can-earn-a-much-higher-income/

Chapter 14

- https://www.bravethinkinginstitute.com/blog/life-transformation/everything-is-created-twice

- Trismegistus, H. and The Three Initiates, *The Emerald Tablet of Hermes & The Kybalion*, Quick Time, 2020, p. 41.

- Allen, J., *As a Man Thinketh*, Martino Fine Books, 2018.

Chapter 15

- https://www.drleaf.com/blogs/news/what-is-the-mind

- Murphy, J., *The Power of Your Subconscious Mind*, Simon & Schuster, 2019.

- https://www.iamfearlesssoul.com/things-you-must-know-about-the-law-of-attraction/

- Trismegistus, H. and The Three Initiates, *The Emerald Tablet of Hermes & The Kybalion*, Quick Time, 2020, p. 42.

Chapter 17

- Canfield, J. and Hansen, M. V., *Chicken Soup for the Soul*, Vermillion, 1998.

Part III

Chapter 18

- Goddard, N., 'Be What You Wish', *Be What You Wish,* Sublime Books, 2015, p. 5.

Chapter 20

- Canfield, J. with Switzer, J., *The Success Principles,* Thorsons, 2017, p. 88.

Part IV

Chapter 25

- Sharma, R., *Who Will Cry When You Die?,* Jaico Publishing House, 2006, pp. 60-61.

- Koran, A., *Bring Out the Magic in Your Mind,* A. Thomas & Co, 1972.

- Sharma, R., *The 5 AM Club,* Harper Thorsons, 2018.

Conclusion

- https://www.proctorgallagherinstitute.com/13079/who-are-you-pretending-to-be

- https://www.youtube.com/watch?v=UF8uR6Z6KLc

Appendix I

- https://unstoppablefoundation.org

In addition to the Reference List, a list of a further nine books follows. Although these nine books have not been referenced, I think you too will find them as precious as I did.

- Bryne, R., *The Secret,* Simon & Schuster, 2006.
- Holliwell, R., *Working with the Law,* DeVross & Company, 2005.
- Nightingale, E., *The Strangest Secret,* Merchant Books, 2013.
- Pritchett, P., *You²*, Pritchett & Associates, 1994.
- Proctor, B., *It's Not About the Money,* G&D Media, 2018.
- Russell, R., *You Too Can Be Prosperous,* DeVross & Company, 2000.
- Sharma, R., *The Monk Who Sold His Ferrari,* Harper Thorsons, 2015.
- Singer, M., *The Untethered Soul,* New Harbinger Publications, 2007.
- Yogananda, P., *Autobiography of a Yogi,* Rupa Publications, 2017.

ACKNOWLEDGMENTS

About 500 years ago, John Donne, the English poet, said that *No man is an island*. And so it has been with the creation of this book. Donne's words remind me of the debt of gratitude I owe to many inspiring people who have made invaluable contributions to the process of writing *Manifest Your Infinite Riches* and the wider cause of the **Centre for Infinite Riches**®.

Some of those I would like to acknowledge are:

Personal Development Practitioners

I feel blessed to have had the opportunity over a number of years to have really delved into the material of three exceedingly well-known philosophers: Jack Canfield, Bob Proctor and Wayne Dyer. Thank you, Bob and Wayne, for the contribution you made to my life when you were still with us and the contribution you continue to make even after your passing. Thank you, Jack, for your belief in the **Centre for Infinite Riches**®, your belief in this book and in my mission and, above all, for actively endorsing my work to your huge audience. I am also grateful to Natalie Ledwell, David Meltzer and Mary Morrissey both for supporting this book, as well as being key messengers, spreading its message far and wide.

The Cast

This book weaves real-life examples with concepts to bring out key learnings in an impactful way. These real-life examples are not only from my own life but also from those of Cat Charlton, Dave Murphy, Alan Howarth, Sunil Kumar, John Assaraf (through Jack Canfield's *The Success Principles*) and Mayra Anand. Thank you for letting me share your stories.

The Publishing Team

To my publisher globally (except in the Indian subcontinent), Cat Charlton, Managing Director at Rowanvale Books, I owe a very special thank you. Not only are you my publisher, who truly exemplifies the meaning of hybrid publishing, but you are also a case study that features prominently in the preceding pages and, most importantly, a dear friend!

No mention of Rowanvale Books would be complete without naming the exceptional team: Alice Hunt for her successful execution of the countless mini design projects within the wider project, Jaide Long for her first level of proofreading, Ellie Owen for the first copy edit, and Alex Mansfield for giving physical form to the design of the front cover.

The Editors

Martin Toseland and Alan Howarth, thank you very much for the structural edits at different parts of the journey spanning more than a year. In particular, Martin, for the many iterations in the final lap that elevated the work to exactly where we wanted, and Alan, for personally trying the methods and permitting me to include your example of how well the methods work.

The Linguists

Lynn Everson and Alex Millward of Lifeline Language Services, I am always thankful to you for a very thorough final proofread of the 35,000 words here. Additionally, Lynn, thank you for being my English-speaking trusted advisor while navigating the world of multilingual translations.

The Beta Readers

Thank you, Naavya Anand and Sangeeta Kapur Anand. Your numerous reads of the first few chapters were indeed invaluable as I iterated and incorporated step by step your extremely helpful comments.

Last, but not least, a special thank you also to Sangeeta (my better half!) for your patience and kindness as I worked rather long hours into most evenings and entire weekends to fulfil my purpose and live my *Dharma*.

CENTRE FOR INFINITE RICHES
Keep Growing . . . . .

Founded by Pushkar Anand after a fifteen-year journey, the **Centre for Infinite Riches**® is a social enterprise with a presence in every continent. The Centre's purpose is to **Uplift Humanity** by enabling everyone it touches to become the person they were always meant to be. You can learn all about the Centre, explore the free content, and check out the courses offered to help you manifest your infinite riches on:

https://www.centreforinfiniteriches.com

rowanvale books

Rowanvale Books is one of the UK's leading hybrid publishers, offering authors the entire gamut of publishing services, tailored to suit each individual author's requirements and budget. These range from stand-alone self-publishing services and customized self-publishing packages to full global sales representation and distribution to leading bookstores. We believe that each author and book is unique and should be treated as such. We deliver a personal, honest and efficient service that allows authors to see their work published, while remaining in control of the process and retaining their creativity. By making publishing services available to authors in a cost-effective and ethical way, we at Rowanvale Books hope to ensure that the local, national and international community benefits from a steady stream of good quality literature.

You can learn all about us, our authors and publications on:

https://www.rowanvalebooks.com